Pests

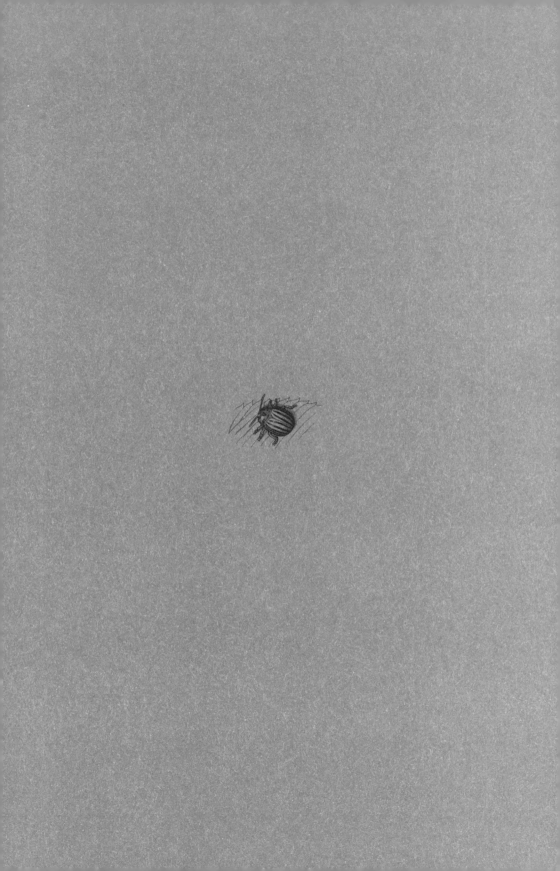

SMITH & HAWKEN

The Hands·On Gardener

Pests

by ELIZABETH *and*
CROW MILLER
with illustrations
by JIM ANDERSON

WORKMAN PUBLISHING·NEW YORK

Library of Congress Cataloging-in-Publication Data
Miller, Elizabeth, 1963–
Pests / by Elizabeth and Crow Miller.
p. cm.—(Smith & Hawken—the hands-on-gardener)
Includes bibliographical references.
ISBN 0-7611-1401-7
1. Garden Pests—Control. 2. Organic gardening. 3. Plants,
Protection of. I. Miller, Crow, II. Title. III. Series.
SB974 .M56 2000
635.9'2'96—dc21
99-086923

Workman Publishing Company, Inc.
708 Broadway
New York, NY 10003-9555

www.workman.com

Manufactured in the United States of America

First printing March 2000

10 9 8 7 6 5 4 3 2 1

CONTENTS

A PESTS PRIMER

The act of creation is different for every gardener. Some people grow only vegetables. Others prefer richly colored flower borders. But all gardeners have one thing in common: a distaste for pests. Our gardens are an expression of creativity and hard work. When insects threaten to destroy our plants, we can easily be tempted to douse them with harmful chemicals. However, if pests invade your garden, there's a reason.

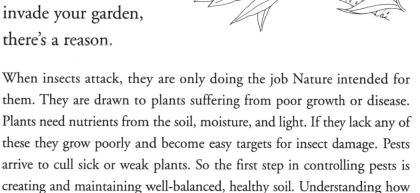

When insects attack, they are only doing the job Nature intended for them. They are drawn to plants suffering from poor growth or disease. Plants need nutrients from the soil, moisture, and light. If they lack any of these they grow poorly and become easy targets for insect damage. Pests arrive to cull sick or weak plants. So the first step in controlling pests is creating and maintaining well-balanced, healthy soil. Understanding how soil feeds your plants is critical when fighting pests without chemicals.

When bugs arrive in your garden, it's tough to remain strictly organic. But you're not doing yourself any favors by using harmful insecticides. When these petrochemicals seep into the soil, they kill nutrient-producing organisms and hamper the soil's ability to feed your plants. They also kill beneficial insects that, if left alone, would attack harmful bugs. In truth, insecticides do more to encourage subsequent pest problems than eliminate them.

In addition to enriching your soil, there are other things you can do to fight insects. For example, you can choose plants that are naturally resistant to pests because of their color, taste, or smell. You can "pair" plants that protect and help each other—called companion planting— which is a sound approach to pest prevention.

The traditional method of crop rotation can also keep your plants from becoming targets for pests and diseases. The process is simple: never plant vegetables or other annuals from the *same family* in the *same location* more than once every three years. Related plants use the same soil nutrients, and pests that lay their eggs nearby get an easy and guaranteed food source. When you rotate your plantings, pests and their offspring die of starvation.

Despite the best preventive measures, every gardener may have pest problems at some point. Luckily, insects are predictable, so you can control them if they do attack. Botanical sprays, oils, and *organic* pesticides are very effective in moderation. Biological controls are safe because each kind is effective against only one class of insect. They don't harm other insects or the environment and are the least toxic controls available. And some home-made sprays and dusts, like biological controls, are selective and target specific critters.

Bad bugs can also be controlled by buying a quantity of good bugs and letting them loose in your garden. Available by mail order, several beneficial insects (from ladybugs to praying mantises and tiny parasitic wasps) can be ordered by the thousand, and they are voracious eaters. But sprays and predatory insects are the last resort. The first line of defense against harmful insects is healthy soil. By avoiding the stress that unbalanced soil imposes on your plants, you can prevent most insect attacks before they happen.

HEALTHY, BALANCED SOIL

Healthy soil is filled with life. You can see larger creatures such as earthworms, springtails, and sowbugs with the naked eye. But equally important are millions of tiny microorganisms that are visible only under a microscope. To get strong, healthy plants you need to build and nourish healthy, balanced soil that will sustain both beneficial insects *and* microorganisms. Once you understand how to create that balance, you can build any soil into a strong, vibrant home for plants that will have a natural resistance to pests and diseases.

In a double handful of rich, organic soil there are as many microorganisms as there are people in the world. These microorganisms include bacteria, fungi, yeasts, molds, and viruses, which are tiny creatures that feed on organic matter, digest it, and make essential nutrients available to your plants. Beneficial microorganisms attack and destroy disease pathogens. Healthy soil not only feeds your plants but also protects them from diseases. Your plants grow strong, drought-resistant root systems and put up a mass of healthy top growth that deters insect attacks.

Chemical fertilizers, pesticides, herbicides—and especially fungicides—destroy this natural food chain in the soil. Plants that are grown in chemically treated soil cannot get the natural nutrients they need, so they have to be fed with artificial nutrients. Instead of being fed by the soil, they become dependent on increasing doses of harmful petrochemicals.

The good news is that apparently dead, lifeless soil can be built into a rich, fertile loam. Yes, built one piece at a time, laid down with care like bricks in a wall. Is your soil too sandy? Rocky? Full of sticky clay? Don't despair; you can turn it into healthy, balanced soil that is filled with life.

Long-lasting results are one benefit of the organic approach to gardening. Chemical fertilizers and other synthetics sometimes produce quick results, but they disappear just as swiftly. Like narcotics, chemicals build total dependence; the need for more and more that they create culminates in a vicious downward spiral. What's worse, they kill the soil's natural ability to feed your plants. They're expensive, too.

There are several ways to encourage and balance the microorganisms in your soil: add compost, use organic soil amendments and blended organic fertilizers, and grow green manure crops. But the absolute first thing you must do without exception is to find out what your soil needs by *soil testing*. Don't waste time and money adding things to your soil until you know what kind you've got, because it'll be guesswork. Call your county's Agricultural Cooperative Extension Service office; they may perform soil analysis tests themselves, but if not they will recommend a commercial soil testing laboratory. Once you've found the right lab, you need to prepare a soil sample for them to test.

PREPARING A SOIL SAMPLE

Depending on the size of your garden, you may want to get more than one soil sample analyzed. The soil in your front flower garden may differ from that in your backyard vegetable garden. The emphasis when preparing a sample is on cleanliness. Be careful not to contaminate the sample with rust, paint, or even sweat from your hands.

Take a clean plastic bucket and a clean, rust-free garden spade. Dig a hole the depth of the spade, then carefully cut a thin slice of soil from the side of the hole and put it in the bucket. Repeat this procedure around your garden, taking soil slices from at least four places. Each slice should include soil from the top surface down to the full depth of the spade.

Testing garden soil is the first—and most important—step when building a garden to withstand pest attacks.

Thoroughly mix the samples together in the bucket, using a large stainless-steel kitchen spoon or a similar implement. From this mixture, fill the container (this may be provided by the testing lab) that you will mail. Label it with your name and address. If you're sending more than one sample for analysis, mark each sample with an identifying location such as "Front yard" or "Bed #1."

Make sure the testing laboratory has a list of what you want your sample tested for (send them a copy of the chart on pages 91–94) so that they provide all the information you need. Tell them what you want to grow there—for example, flowers, shrubs, vegetables. When you get the results back, compare them with the desired levels shown in the chart on pages 91–94.

BUILDING HEALTHY SOIL

Once you have the results of your soil analysis, you can use that knowledge to start building good garden soil. Resist the temptation to add more than the recommended amounts of things: *balance* is what you want, and too much of anything can upset that balance.

It takes Nature more than 500 years to form an inch of soil. The same chemical, physical, and biological forces that formed soil eons ago are still creating it today. Decaying plant matter, climate, glacial forces, and the action of microorganisms are still at work. All the gardener does is help the process along by nurturing the natural forces to create a harmonious balance. Soil improvement can be broken into three categories: organic content, acidity and nutrients, and soil structure. All of these need to work together to create healthy soil.

ORGANIC CONTENT

This is the first item to look at on the soil analysis because it tells you how much humus (organic content) you've got. As you can see from the comparison chart (see page 91), the *minimum* desired level is 5 percent. If yours is less than this, don't worry, you're not alone. Most gardens in need of help show a level of 1 or 2 percent, sometimes less. Using the chart, calculate how much compost or vegetative matter you need to add to bring it up to the right level.

If your soil is seriously deficient in humus, adding a large amount of mature, fully rotted compost is a quick fix. You may have to buy this until your own compost heaps fill your needs (see pages 12 to 14). A

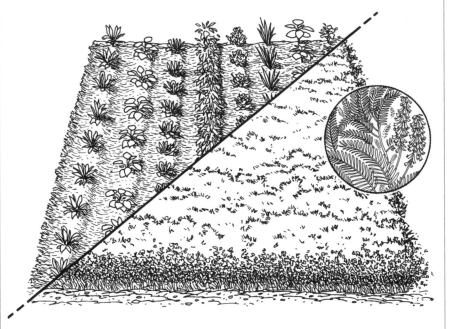

Cover crops like vetch are a good choice for soils in need of rehab because they encourage a range of biological activity.

compromise can be had by adding less compost, then planting a cover crop, often called a green manure.

COVER CROPS: Green manure is an odd name, but it describes a process that's as old as farming. All it means is sowing the seed of a plant, letting it grow, then tilling or digging it in so that it decomposes in the soil. Even farmers who use lots of chemicals plant green manure "cover crops," such as winter rye, which not only anchor the soil against winter erosion but add large amounts of vegetative matter when they're plowed under in spring.

For the gardener, there are several terrific green manures that are fast and easy to grow. Many of them are very attractive plants, so you don't need to worry about your garden looking a mess while they're doing their thing. Some have odd names, too, like hairy vetch *(Vicia villosa);* in reality, it's a pretty plant with ferny leaves and charming purple-blue flowers. It is a member of the pea family, a legume, which means that it performs a double service for you. While the tops are twining and tumbling over their own lush green growth (and the flowers are feeding bees and butterflies), the roots are fixing nitrogen in the soil. Other possibilities include common vetch *(Vicia sativa),* and purple vetch *(Vicia atropurpurea).* These green manures grow dense enough to defeat most weeds and fast enough to beat bugs. They also improve the drainage of your soil with their deep roots. And finally, when you till or dig them in (before they go to seed unless you want a repeat performance), they add large amounts of organic matter.

This raw vegetative matter disintegrates as soil organisms feed on it and convert it into materials that nourish plant growth. This biological activity helps the structure of the soil, which is so important for admitting oxygen and water and for root growth. As they enrich the soil, green manures transform a plot that is too sandy or too compacted into fertile land.

Buckwheat, oats, rye, clovers, and vetches are good green manures. Organic seed can be purchased by mail order. But if you're buying seed at a farm store (farmers call green manures "cover crops"), make sure you get *untreated* seed. Many agricultural seeds are treated with chemicals you don't want in your garden. However, if you're planting clovers, vetches, or any other members of the pea and bean (legume) family, you should buy some bacterial inoculant for the particular species you intend to grow. Legumes work in harmony with rhizobacteria that live on their roots. It is a symbiotic relationship, and it's these rhizobacteria that take gaseous nitrogen from the air and fix it as nitrogen in the soil. Rhizobacteria exist naturally in the soil, but not in sufficient quantities to maximize nitrogen fixation. By adding some to the seed you sow, you ensure healthy top and root growth.

A good seed catalog will help you find a green manure suitable for your area of the country. Some companies offer soil-builder seed mixes just for this purpose. Peaceful Valley Farm Supply (see Resources, pages 95–97) has a mix that they claim yields up to 290 pounds of nitrogen and 49 tons of organic matter per acre!

ACIDITY is very important. Your soil analysis will show the pH, or relative level of acidity, of your soil. Levels of pH are measured on a scale from 0 to 14. From 0 to 7 is acidic, and from 7 to 14 is alkaline. Neutral is 7. Plants have different pH requirements. For example, most vegetables like a slightly acidic soil in the range from 6.5 to 6.8. Rhododendrons and conifers do best in soil that's around 6.0. Lawn grass prefers a neutral to slightly alkaline soil, 7.0 to 7.5.

Adjust pH levels carefully. To "sweeten" soil that is too acidic, add dolomitic limestone at the rate recommended on the bag. To correct excess alkalinity, add sulfur in the form of gypsum or iron sulfate.

NUTRIENT levels and balance are vital to your plants' health and ability to fight off insect attacks. The major nutrients are nitrogen, phosphorus, and potassium, known by the chemical symbols N, P, and K. Secondary nutrients are calcium, magnesium, sulfur, sodium, and hydrogen. The micronutrients are zinc, manganese, iron, copper, boron, and molybdenum. You may find it surprising, but all these things have to be present in healthy soil, and in the right amounts! It is almost certain that you will have to correct nutrient imbalances. But make sure you do it organically, buying what you need from one of the suppliers listed in Resources. Finally, apply amendments at *no more than* the recommended rate.

WHAT IS SOIL MADE OF?

Clay, silt, sand, and humus (organic matter) are the four basic ingredients of soil. Clay particles are the smallest. A heavy clay soil is almost impervious to water because the tiny particles cling tightly together. Silt particles are slightly larger and permit some drainage. They are composed of mostly primary minerals and are present in the richest soils. Sand particles are the largest; very sandy soils cannot hold water or nutrients.

Humus (pronounced hew-muss) is decayed plant matter, rich in nutrients and essential for a healthy, friable soil. Compost, when it it so fully decayed that its constituents can no longer be identified, becomes humus, as do fallen leaves and other plant residues such as roots of dead plants.

The ideal garden soil contains balanced amounts of clay, silt, sand, and humus. Clay and silt provide essential minerals and trace elements. Sand helps the soil to drain properly (as gardeners say, it keeps it "open"). And humus holds water and nutrients in the top few inches of soil where plant roots feed.

SOIL STRUCTURE

Your soil analysis will tell you what soil you have. As you do with nutrient levels, make changes carefully and don't be tempted to overdo it. Sand *and* compost will leaven heavy clay soils. Clay *and* compost will benefit sandy soils. Compost *and* a green manure crop will help any kind of soil.

A common soil structure problem is compaction. If your plants look sick, but you are unable to identify the cause, compaction may be the culprit. Wet, poorly drained soil is prone to compaction. The soils around new houses are often compacted by heavy construction equipment. Even your own footsteps in a much-trodden garden can pack the soil down so that air is excluded. Plant roots need oxygen, which they can't get in compacted soil.

ARE YOUR PLANTS STARVING?

If you remember the connection between plant health and insects, you will be able to establish a healthy balance in your garden. Spotting the symptoms of nutritional deficiency in your plants will give you a head start in preventing insect damage. Following are the most common symptoms.

NITROGEN

Deficiency: Slow growth and slender, fibrous stems; foliage and stems turn yellow; trees will grow small, pale leaves.
Solution: Fish emulsion foliage spray or root feeding, dried blood meal, or aged chicken manure will quickly correct nitrogen deficiency. Compost and succulent green manure crops work well, too.
Excess: Lots of large, dark green leaves with long stems; flowering/ fruiting will be delayed.
Solution: Add carbon to the soil in the form of sawdust or shredded dead leaves.

SULFUR

Deficiency: New, young leaves turn pale green or yellow, while older leaves remain green.
Solution: Dig in moisture-retaining humus; seaweed is particularly good.

PHOSPHORUS

Deficiency: Leaves usually small, erect, and dark green; leaves may turn dull green and have purplish tints in later stages; older leaves often dark brown to almost black; fruit and seed production reduced.
Solution: In acid soils, apply lime and bonemeal; in alkaline soils, add humus and bonemeal. Rock phosphorus is slow but lasts a long time.

POTASSIUM

Deficiency: Scorched appearance along older leaf margins; weak stalks that sometimes collapse; legumes will slowly drop all leaves.
Solution: Add compost, seaweed meal or wood ash. Seaweed mulch, granite dust, or greensand release potassium for years.

BORON

Deficiency: Poor growth of tops and roots; the underside of some leaves may turn reddish-purple; terminal buds are brittle; inter- nodes (the distance from one leaf to the next) become short. Celery leaves become brown and mottled; cauliflower curds will appear water soaked, then turn brown.

Solution: Spray with a fish-seaweed solution, and water the soil with a solution of 1 tablespoon of borax to 1 gallon of water. In acid soil, dig in seaweed or composted leaves.

CALCIUM

Deficiency: Growing points discolored; young leaves severely distorted and show a hooked tip; in tomatoes, stems, leaves, and fruiting branches die back, and fruit shows blossom-end rot; legumes show pale green leaves with dead margins; pods are few and poorly developed; tip leaves have a scorched and ragged appearance; leaf margins roll inward.

Solution: Dig in finely ground limestone or gypsum, and compost.

COPPER

Deficiency: Leaves lose vigor and turn bluish-green before becoming pale green and yellow (called chlorosis). Plants may fail to flower. There is excessive leaf shedding, and seed heads droop.

Solution: Spray foliage and feed roots with fish-seaweed emulsion. In acid soil, dig in seaweed or composted leaves.

IRON

Deficiency: Young leaves yellow while veins remain green; leaf tips appear dry and scorched; on trees, dieback may extend to whole branches.

Solution: Iron may be present but unavailable because soil is too alkaline. Check your soil pH and add sulfur or peat moss, and compost.

MAGNESIUM

Deficiency: Leaves turn pale green, then yellow; corn shows streaks on lower leaves; flower and vegetable leaves turn yellow with reddish-purple color at the tips and margins, then curl upward.

Solution: Dig in finely ground dolomitic limestone. Fish-seaweed emulsion spray is also good.

ZINC

Deficiency: Leaves turn yellow, die, and drop off. Bean pods may drop. Leaves grow thick and close together.

Solution: Spray with fish-seaweed solution.

Adding compost, and if it is lacking, sand, will do the trick. You may need to double-dig the garden as well, digging down to twice the depth of a fork or spade. Deep rototilling may help, but most tillers don't go deep enough to alleviate serious compaction.

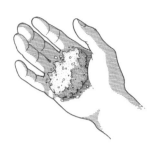

A simple "hand test" can often reveal whether soil contains sand clay or silt.

Grab a handful to find out what your soil is made of, get right down and feel it. Loosen the top of the soil with a garden fork. Spread some soil in the palm of your hand and run your fingers over it. If the sample is dry and feels like cake flour, or is wet and feels smooth, it is fairly high in silt. Dry clay feels harsh; wet clay feels sticky and greasy. If it feels gritty, it is probably sand.

Another test can be done with a glass jar that has a screw-on lid. Half-fill it with soil, first removing any pebbles, and add water, leaving about an inch of space at the top. Screw on the lid, and shake the contents vigorously. Let it sit on a shelf for two days.

Without moving it, look at the layers that have settled out. Sand, the coarsest particles, will be at the bottom. Above that will be silt, topped with clay. Finally, if you are lucky, there will be a layer of dark humus, some of which may float on the surface. The water may still be cloudy with minute particles, but you can see, at a glance, what proportion of each element is in the sample. If you repeat this test with soil from different parts of your garden, you will probably find a few variations. These quick-and-dirty tests show you what makes up your soil.

MAKING COMPOST

Compost is the gardener's friend. It lightens heavy clay soils and provides plant nutrients. It works like a sponge to absorb and hold moisture. And by stimulating beneficial microbial life, it helps prevent plant diseases. Despite the earlier caution about using too much of anything, it's hard to imagine having too much compost. Most gardeners never have enough, so if you haven't made compost before, now's the time to start.

Adding compost is a simple and rewarding task.

A compost heap can be no more than a simple unenclosed pile in a corner of your garden where you toss material. Left alone it will become compost in about a year. However, such a pile won't produce as much compost as you are likely to need, and it takes too long to do it.

Compost is best made in some sort of enclosure. It should be at least 3 feet across. It can be made of metal posts and chicken wire, a circle of wire lath (available from a mason supply yard), or a purchased compost bin, many of which are made from recycled plastics. "Biostack" composters have three horizontal sections that nest on each other, making it easy to turn the pile. Last, you'll need at least two compost bins.

FEEL THE HEAT: To get lots of microbial action going, compost needs carbon and nitrogen. Carbon comes from brown, dead material such as leaves. Nitrogen comes from green material like grass clippings. Try to get roughly three or four parts carbon to one part of nitrogen. Build the pile until it's at least 3 feet deep, moistening the layers as you add material. It should not be wet—aim for the consistency of a wrung-out sponge. Sprinkle some garden soil among the layers to introduce extra microorganisms.

COMPOST INGREDIENTS

Compost has three requirements: a supply of suitable material, moisture, and air. If you look around, you will find plenty of material. Leaves, grass clippings, and yard waste are the main ingredients, to which you can add vegetable scraps from the kitchen, seaweed, manure (cow, horse, chicken, or rabbit—avoid cat, dog, and human feces), straw, woodchips, sawdust, and some garden soil. Avoid adding weeds that are bearing seeds. If you want to make a lot of compost quickly, a chipper-shredder is a great help. It breaks material into smaller pieces and gets the process started faster.

Within a couple of days, your pile will heat up to as much as 160°F. This is the result of microbial action and indicates a good, working pile. When the heat subsides, or after about a week, *turn* the pile into a new heap. With a garden or compost fork, take the top of the pile and toss it into the bottom of your second bin. Try to bring material from the outside of the old pile into the middle of the new pile. If it's dry, moisten it with a watering can or hose spray as you go. Fluff it, don't pack it down, as the pile needs oxygen.

After a day or so, the new pile should heat up again as the hungry microbes find new material to feed on. If it doesn't, mix in some more green material. Turn it once a week and you will see a garden miracle as it happens. Gradually, the ingredients will break down and become hard to identify. In 6 to 8 weeks, you'll have compost!

MULCH helps to improve soil structure and retain moisture. Several organic mulch materials are available. On flower beds and pathways, woodchips work well. In vegetable gardens, seaweed, a thick layer of straw, or shredded leaves help cool the soil in hot weather, and when they have rotted down you can dig or till them in to add organic matter. Avoid hay, as it can contain weed seeds. Dried (not fresh) grass clippings are rich in nitrogen and help most plants. Finally, pine needles are acidic, break down slowly, and are perfect for acid-loving small fruits and ornamental plants.

REALITY CHECK: TISSUE ANALYSIS

It is possible for you to do almost everything correctly and still have plants that just don't look right. There is no apparent insect damage, but there is an imbalance somewhere. You should be especially concerned if a whole family of your plants is sickly—peas and beans, for example, or potatoes, tomatoes, and eggplants. This could mean that this group of plants is not getting something it needs or is getting too much of something. You may need to change its diet.

However, check the soil pH level first. Maybe all the good things you added to your soil changed the pH balance, which might have "locked up" some necessary nutrients. You can easily check the pH yourself with a little testing kit available at most garden centers or by mail order. If the pH is where it should be, the next step in finding out what's wrong is tissue analysis.

Check with the lab that did your soil analysis, your Agricultural Cooperative Extension Service, or a good local nursery to find the right laboratory. Ask how you should prepare samples for mailing. When you get the results, compare them with the chart on page 91. Perhaps there is a potassium deficiency, or one or more trace elements are in short supply. Perhaps a nutrient is unavailable to your plants, even though lots of it is in the soil, because it is "locked up" or being blocked by an absence or excess of something else. It is usually easy to correct the problem once you have identified it, and your next crop will reward you with glowing good health.

Not only will you have learned something vital about your soil and your plants, you will have achieved balance. It is a deeply satisfying feeling. Balancing the soil so that it provides what your plants need will reduce insect damage by as much as 80 percent.

WHY SOIL NUTRIENTS ARE IMPORTANT

Lettuce, spinach, and Swiss chard are foliage crops—we harvest their leaves. Foliage crops' primary need is an abundance of nitrogen to encourage leaf growth. They also need high amounts of calcium and magnesium and adequate trace amounts of iron. By contrast, root crops such as carrots, onions, and beets need very little nitrogen but plenty of phosphorus and potassium. And plants that flower and produce fruit—annual and perennial flowers, and vegetables such as tomatoes, eggplants, squash, and beans—need a moderate amount of nitrogen and an adequate supply of phosphorus and potassium.

It is important to remember that an overabundance of nutrients can be as bad as a shortage. Don't be tempted to think that twice as much will be twice as good. It doesn't work that way—balance is essential! Healthy vegetables, fed by healthy soil, are good for you, too. When we eat plants, the nutrients they take up are passed on to us in the form of vitamins and minerals.

CHOOSING THE BEST PLANTS

Rich, balanced soil is the first essential. The next step is to choose healthy plants and minimize any environmental stresses that might weaken them. Remember, weak plants *attract* insect pests.

Plants that have been grown from pure seed and carefully nurtured during their growth stand a good chance of remaining healthy throughout their lives. But plants that have been mass-produced with constant chemical inputs are weak from the outset and despite the most loving organic treatment will never develop their full potential.

Plant genetics are influenced by evolution. For example, if seed is taken from plants that have, for generations, been overwatered, they will grow into plants with shallow, drought-prone root systems. But if seed is saved from plants that have been sparingly watered for years, they will have long roots that search out moisture deep in the earth and will withstand occasional dry periods.

Plants that are raised using synthetic fertilizers receive only the major nutrients and never get the secondary nutrients and trace elements needed for healthy, balanced growth. Continued use of pesticides and fungicides weakens the plant's natural ability to fight off insect and disease attacks. The plant's immune system is irreparably damaged.

Whenever possible, use untreated and certified organic seeds. Better still, save your own seeds

LESSON OF WEEDS

Weeds are a perfect example of the value of strong genes. They grow wherever Nature puts them, no one waters or fertilizes them, they suffer little or no insect damage, and they flourish (as every gardener knows!). How? Why?

The answer is simple. Because weeds have never been genetically altered to suit human needs; their original, primal genetic structure remains intact. All plants once grew wild and strong. But the plants humans have chosen to domesticate, modify, and grow in their gardens have become weaker, more susceptible to drought, disease, and insect damage. A weed, after all, is just a successful plant growing in the wrong place.

from plants grown organically. Using organic seeds will help control harmful insects in your garden by producing strong plants. Grow only open-pollinated (or "heirloom") varieties. Their seeds breed true to their parents. Seeds taken from a hybrid plant are unpredictable and may revert to one or the other of its parents. By saving seeds of heirloom varieties from your own organic garden, you know that the parent plants were healthy, vigorous, and productive—and that the seeds are fresh.

ENVIRONMENTAL STRESS

Healthy soil can prevent about 80 percent of insect damage. A strong plant's genes can fight off another 10 percent. Environmental stress, which is obviously harder for a gardener to control, accounts for the final 10 percent. Plants are vulnerable to insect attack when they are stressed by temperature extremes, wind chill, drought, overwatering, transplant shock, air pollution, and acid rain.

You can't control or accurately predict long-term weather conditions, but in the same way that you can help fight off colds and infections by taking vitamins, you can strengthen your plants with foliar feeding—spraying the leaves with an emulsion mixture of fish and seaweed extract. Dilute your mixture with water according to the instructions on the container. A foliar feeding program can control environmental stress by boosting your plants' growth potential in a natural way. The results will amaze you.

There are three situations in which foliar feeding is most valuable. First, during transplanting—when seedlings are moved from a protected growing environment into the open garden—plants are at risk. Seedlings that initially wilt after transplanting will appear to recover within a day or so, but this transplant shock can set the plant back by as much as two weeks. That's how long it takes for a

Diluted foliar sprays can be an effective deterrent to insect attacks.

seedling to adjust to its new environment. Avoid transplant shock by dunking leaves, roots, and all—into a fish-seaweed solution.

Foliar feeding also proves its worth during very low temperatures. As nights become cooler, tomatoes and other heat-loving crops should be sprayed once a week with a fish-seaweed solution. This will keep them producing right up until the first hard frost.

If this seems hard to believe, try an experiment next fall. Spray *half* of your tomato patch with a fish-seaweed solution. As nighttime temperatures drop, the unsprayed plants will stop flowering and producing fruit, but the sprayed plants will continue to fruit. When the first light frost hits, the unsprayed plants will die while the rest of your plants continue to grow. Only a hard frost will finally kill them.

Drought is the third stress threat. It can be avoided with the help of foliar spraying, a drip irrigation system, and moisture-conserving mulch. Drought often accompanies high temperatures, and plants need moisture for transpiration. This process is similar in its effect to human perspiration—it helps cool the plant down.

Spray your plants once a week with a fish-seaweed solution, and lay a drip irrigation system between the rows; run it until the ground is moist

(not wet) to a depth of about 6 inches. Drip irrigation conserves water and puts it where plants need it, at their roots. Sprinklers encourage disease and waste huge amounts of water. Finally, a layer of mulch helps the soil stay moist and cool.

A simple fish-seaweed solution sprayed on leaves will give your plants added life and productivity.

By doing all you can to control soil imbalance, plant genetics, and environmental stress, you strengthen your plants' natural defenses against insect invasions and diseases. Under ideal conditions, you should not lose any more than 2 or 3 percent of your plants to injurious insects. Even so, you should expect to find a few bad bugs in your garden—they provide a food source for beneficial insects. Your goal as an organic gardener is to create a healthy, *balanced* growing environment.

Outwitting Insects

The best way to deal with pests is to know them and how they work. Some pests appear smart, but once you know what attracts them, what does not—and what actually repels them—you can outwit them with ease. It only seems difficult because insect pests have had generations of experience in evading predators, and you're just getting started. You need to know which insects are enemies (relatively few), and which are friends (most of them).

Insects react to instinct and evolution. Because many of them breed quickly and in large numbers, they can adapt quickly to threats. This is why chemical insecticides are virtually useless: insects can rapidly evolve resistant strains to survive a toxic onslaught. If you take steps to *prevent* insects from attacking your garden, you'll be way ahead of the game.

There are several ways to do this. Insects are sensitive to color, smell, and taste. Anything you can do to confuse them works to your advantage. It is said that a Colorado potato beetle can recognize the unique green color of a potato or eggplant from a long distance. A whole field of those plants is obviously a prime target. Japanese beetles home in on their favorite foods, from roses and other ornamentals to vegetable crops. But if your plants are camouflaged and protected by other plant species that bugs aren't interested in or that actively repel them, they're more likely to look elsewhere for an easy meal.

Many insects have taste sensors in their feet, so if they land on a plant that repels them (such as a marigold), they'll leave the area in a hurry. If you surround your most insect-sensitive plants with species unattractive to pests, they will probably give your garden a miss.

You can sidestep most insect problems before they begin by avoiding large blocks of susceptible plants, interplanting with resistant or repellent species, and of course strengthening your plants by giving them good, healthy soil in which to grow. However, don't panic and rush for the insecticide spray whenever you see a "bad" bug. A few will do little damage and will provide food for their predators. Your aim as an organic gardener is to create a fine and harmonious balance. Most insects are welcome visitors to any garden. Others need to be carefully watched lest they become a problem. It helps to know something about them.

KNOW YOUR ENEMY

Creatures with jointed legs are known as arthropods. This grouping includes lobsters, crabs, spiders, millipedes—and insects. Insects and some other arthropods have exoskeletons, or an armored exterior skeleton. The distinguishing features of insects are that they all have six legs and are cold-blooded.

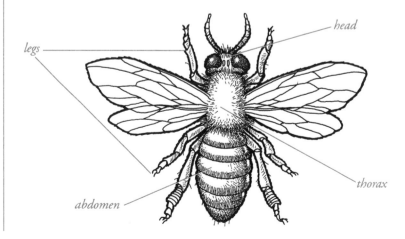

Mature insects have segmented bodies with three parts: head, thorax, and abdomen. Their bodies are often protected by waxy secretions or other substances emitted through tiny pores. The exoskeleton is made of chitin (pronounced ky-tin), which is so tough that even the digestive juices of mammals cannot break it down.

Insects' eyes are sensitive to colors, particularly those of their food targets. The design of an insect's mouth is suited to the food it eats. Mouthparts either chew, bore, or suck. Sucking insects have a beak through which they draw their liquid sustenance.

THE GOOD GUYS

Most insects are either harmless or beneficial. Carnivorous insects eat other arthropods and are divided into two groups: predators and parasites. The best-known predator is the humble little lady beetle or ladybug; both it and its larvae have voracious appetites. They can devour a complete infestation of aphids in a very short time. Most people are familiar with the ladybug, but you should learn to recognize its larvae, too. They are ugly little beasts, but they eat even more than the adults.

Another predator with a large appetite is the praying mantis. Less finicky than the ladybug, it will eat anything it can catch, including a few beneficial insects and even other mantises (the female often kills and eats the male after they have mated, unless he makes a quick getaway). By contrast, a predator with a very limited menu is the aphid midge, which eats only aphids.

Parasitic insects (called parasitoids) lay their eggs near, on, or

FRIEND OR FOE?

Learn to recognize bad bugs *and* good bugs. Some are easy to confuse. The friendly ladybug isn't much different from the positively hateful Mexican bean beetle. The rove beetle eats several harmful pests, yet is easily confused with the destructive earwig. The spined soldier bug eats damaging caterpillars, but looks very similar to the brown stinkbug, a pest. Chapter 3 deals with insect identification.

A few insects are your enemies, but you'll find that most are your friends.

even in other insects. When the larvae hatch they devour the host insect. If you see a tomato hornworm—a very large green caterpillar with a pointed "horn" on its tail—that is studded all over its body with white

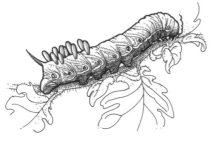

ovals like grains of rice, it has been attacked by a parasitic wasp. The white ovals are the wasp's eggs, and you shouldn't squash the caterpillar because it will soon die. And the tiny parasitic wasps that will hatch and feed on it are the next generation of beneficial insects that will protect your garden.

The wasp eggs attached to this caterpillar's back will soon hatch and consume him.

OUTTHINKING YOUR ENEMY

Some plants have developed a natural resistance to insects and diseases, and many hybrid plants are bred to resist, or at least tolerate, environmental conditions or diseases. Seed catalog listings include information about resistance or tolerance. Look for codes that indicate resistance, such as *BMV* (bean mosaic virus), *V* (verticillium wilt), or "tolerance to black rot." Tolerant plants may suffer some damage, but will regenerate tissue fast enough to remain healthy and defy insect attack.

Because it can take more than one season to create healthy soil, these resistant varieties can help you make the transition and protect your crop

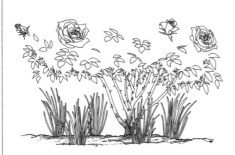

from insects. Once your soil is in better shape, you can plant strong heirloom varieties that will be able to defend themselves.

You may notice that while some plants are completely infested by insects, others have no problems at all. Many plants are simply uninteresting to insects because of their taste or smell, while others actively *repel* insects.

Numerous species of the onion family are excellent pest deterrents. For example, chives interplanted with roses will help repel aphids.

Consider planting a repellent species next to plants that insects love. The repellent plant may not keep every insect away (although it might), but it will deter most of them. Plan your garden to take advantage of this, particularly while you are making the transition to healthy soil and healthy plants.

The whole onion family—onions, chives, leeks, garlic, and shallots—are great deterrents, and need not be restricted to the vegetable garden. Egyptian onions are quite ornamental and will repel peach tree borers, beetles, and aphids. Chives look good around roses, and also repel aphids. Garlic is the most powerful of the group and will benefit the garden wherever you plant it.

Easy to grow and pretty, marigolds repel pests when they are planted between rows in a vegetable garden and as borders around flower beds. A ring of marigolds around a susceptible ornamental will surround it with natural protection. Marigold roots emit substances that will rid your garden of destructive nematodes, and their pungent odor repels such hard-to-deter pests as Mexican bean beetles and even rabbits. Dwarf French marigolds are very compact, don't sprawl or sag, and stay tidy all summer. Plant them around the base of staked tomatoes, trellised cucumbers or squash, bell peppers, and tender annual flowers for maximum protection.

A few pests such as cutworms and snails will attack marigolds, but they are easy to circumvent. A toothpick right next to the stem,

PROTECTIVE HERBS

Herbs can be very effective in repelling insects. Most have strong aromas and even stronger tastes, so it's easy to understand why bugs avoid them. Attractive and useful plants in their own right, they shouldn't be restricted to the herb garden. Basil, for example, vigorously protects tomatoes against several pests, and it's an excellent fly repellent.

Summer savory protects all kinds of beans. The Mexican bean beetle, an energetic and destructive pest, leaves the area immediately when savory is planted there. Sage and mint protect cabbage, broccoli, cauliflower, kohlrabi, and Brussels sprouts. And mustard, itself a member of the cabbage (brassica) family, will attract the harlequin bug away from your cabbage crops.

or a paper collar pressed into the soil around it will stop cutworms. A few saucers of beer, cider, or sugar water will trap snails and slugs. Replace the liquid every day or two, or after rain, and you will soon rid your garden of these pests.

Other flowers that discourage insects include dahlias, coreopsis, cosmos, asters, and chrysanthemums. Petunias do a surprisingly good job of protecting apple and other fruit trees. Feverfew seems absolutely bug-proof, and painted daisies work as a positive deterrent. If you grow your own pyrethrum daisies, they will protect your plants while they are growing, and you can collect and dry the flower heads to make your own pyrethrin insecticide. Grind the dried material, mix it with water, strain, and spray. Be careful with this, however: some people are allergic to pyrethrins, and because it is a broad-spectrum insecticide it can kill beneficial insects as well as the bad guys. If you use it at all, use it sparingly—don't drench the whole area with it.

CROP ROTATION

If you plant a flower or vegetable species in the same spot every year, you're guaranteeing pests an easy meal. Many pests feed on a plant and then lay eggs or pupate in the soil below. Winter comes and goes. When enough time has elapsed and the weather warms up again, the

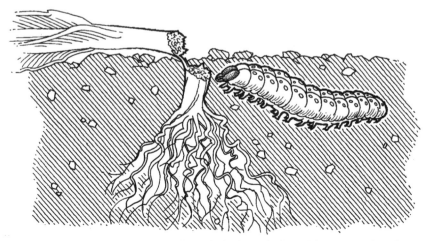

Crop rotation insures against a ready-made food supply for soil-borne pests from last year's garden crop.

RELATED PLANTS ATTRACT SIMILAR PESTS

Plants within the same family tend to attract similar pests. For example, cabbage, cauliflower, broccoli, Brussels sprouts, kale, and radish are all members of the brassica (mustard) family. Cabbage looper caterpillars and cabbage maggots love them all. Tomatoes, eggplant, peppers, and potatoes are all nightshades. Hornworms and Japanese beetles think every one is delicious.

Some relationships are even more surprising. Sweet corn and popcorn are grasses. Asparagus is a lily. Onions, leeks, shallots, chives, and garlic are part of the amaryllis family. Rhubarb is related to buckwheat. Beets, chard, and spinach are members of the goosefoot clan. And who could guess that carrots, celery, parsnips, and dill are all members of the parsley family?

Other relationships are easier to see: pumpkin, squash, cucumber, cantaloupe, watermelon, and muskmelon are all gourds. And lettuce, chicory, and endive are members of the composite family.

If you remember these family ties you will be able to keep insect pests guessing by growing close relatives in different locations every year.

larvae emerge and start crawling around looking for food. If you have planted their favorite food nearby, their objective is accomplished.

But if you move your plantings around every year—never putting the same species in the same spot more than once every three to five years—the larvae emerge and find no food. They'll wander around for a while, but without the immediate protection of their target food they're likely to get eaten by one of your natural friends, such as birds, toads, or predatory insects.

Changing the location of plants every year requires some planning. Most gardens are limited in size, and we all want borders filled with flowers and a vegetable garden bursting with bounty. However, even moving something 10 or 12 feet next year will help, and most of us can manage that. Many gardeners now use raised beds because it is easier to control soil quality. A garden that is divided into separate beds makes it easier.

Make a detailed sketch of your layout, noting plant locations. Graph paper helps to keep things roughly to scale. Then during the winter, when gardeners dream of spring, plan the next season's garden layout. Try to move species, and the other members of that plant family, as far as possible from their last location.

AVOID MONOCULTURE

Planting a large crop of single (or related) species is called monoculture, and it is the greatest cause of harmful insect infestations. As an organic grower, you should plant a diversified crop. Polyculture, or variety, should be your target. Instead of planting just one crop, interplant different crops.

For example, plant corn in widely spaced rows. Then, when the corn is about knee-high, plant two Kentucky Wonder pole bean seeds at the base of each plant. As they grow, train the beans around the corn stalks. Beans are a legume, so they fix nitrogen in the soil. This helps the corn, which needs lots of nitrogen to grow tall and straight. Finally, between the rows of corn and beans, plant a bush summer squash. This will grow into a living mulch to shade the soil from drying sun and keep weeds to a minimum.

If your hyacinth, narcissus, or other bulbs are threatened by nematodes, interplant marigolds along the edges and throughout your flower beds. They emit a substance from their roots that will attract the nematodes; but once there, they will be unable to lay their eggs. And if you treat marigolds as a green manure crop, digging or tilling them under in the soil, they will keep nematodes away for years. Some seed suppliers, such as Johnny's Selected Seeds (Albion, Maine), sell marigold seed by the pound, which is *much* cheaper than buying it in little packets. Asparagus is also said to kill nematodes. Its beautiful, ferny foliage would not be out of place in any flower garden—and you would have the benefit of eating it, too!

COMPANION PLANTING

For centuries, farmers and gardeners practiced companion planting because they found that some plants seemed to help others growing in the same vicinity. Occasionally, one plant appears to reap all the benefits, but other combinations seem to help both plants. Often, one plant simply helps repel insects from another, which is easy to understand. Sometimes, though, they just seem to like each other's company.

Some plants definitely *do not* get along together, and one or both will sicken and even die if they are too close. For example, apple trees release volatile substances that inhibit the development of potato seedlings. In return, the potato seedlings produce a toxin that can build up in the soil and cause chemical imbalances in young apple trees. Avoid planting fennel and wormwood in your garden as they are toxic to other plants! Be mindful of your plants' enemies and plant only friends together.

Asparagus is helped by tomatoes, parsley, and basil, as they repel asparagus beetles. **Beans** like potatoes, rosemary, and marigolds because they deter beetles. Beans

Companion plants, like beets and bush beans, work together to repel insects and foster growth.

also do well with carrots, cucumbers, cauliflower, and cabbage. **Beets** grow well near bush beans, onions, and kohlrabi, but are turned off by pole beans. **Cabbage** pests are discouraged by potatoes, celery, dill, chamomile, sage, thyme, mint, pennyroyal, lavender, beets, and onions. Other aromatics that offend cabbage pests include oregano, catnip, hyssop, and rosemary, which deter moths that beget caterpillars. **Carrots** are helped by peas, lettuce, chives, onions, leeks, rosemary, sage, parsley, and tomatoes (sage and parsley repel carrot fly). But don't plant dill near carrots. **Catnip** is excellent for border plantings as it protects against flea beetles. **Chives** do well near carrots, and, if planted at the base of the trunks, help fruit trees avoid climbing insects.

Corn likes potatoes, peas, beans, cucumbers, pumpkins, and squash. **Cucumbers** go well with corn, beans, peas, radishes, and sunflowers, but dislike potatoes; tansy will deter cucumber beetles and squash bugs. **Garlic** does well near roses and raspberries, and will deter Japanese beetles and other pests throughout the garden. Plant **horseradish** with potatoes and around plum trees to discourage plum curculio.

Jerusalem artichokes do well with corn. Plant **leeks** with onions, celery, and carrots. **Lettuce** likes carrots, radishes, strawberries, and cucumbers. **Lovage** helps all plants repel pests, and **marigolds** discourage insects and soil nematodes. **Nasturtium** planted near tomatoes, radishes, cabbage, and under fruit trees deters aphids and will keep pests away from cucumbers, squash, and pumpkins.

Onions will flourish among your beets, strawberries, tomatoes, lettuce, and summer savory, but keep them away from peas and beans. **Peas** do well with beans, caraway, carrots, and corn, and mint helps growth and flavor, but peas actively dislike garlic and onions. **Potatoes** like horseradish (active against blister beetles), beans, corn, cabbage, marigolds, and eggplant, but don't do well near pumpkins, squash, cucumbers, tomatoes, raspberries, or sunflowers. **Pumpkins** like melons, squash, and corn. **Spinach** does well with strawberries and any member of the cabbage family. For **squash**, plant borage to improve growth and flavor, and pink petunias to deter borers. Squash and potatoes, however, don't get along. Among **strawberries**, plant thyme to prevent worms

HOW TIMED PLANTING BEAT THE POTATO BUGS

Several decades ago, potato farmers on Long Island knew very little about soil testing or the wants and needs of plants. Organic fertilizers and soil amendments were not on the market. Farmers rotated their crops, manured their fields, and grew green-manure cover crops.

On Long Island, potatoes traditionally were planted in late March and harvested in mid-July, and Colorado potato beetles regularly devastated the crops. One farmer observed that the potato beetles emerged in mid-June. So he decided to prepare his fields and plant his potatoes in October. He mulched the seedlings with straw to protect them from frosts. His plants started growing again in March, having already established good root systems the previous fall. And he was able to harvest his entire crop by the end of May, before the potato beetles appeared.

The best plan of attack is often no attack at all. By observing the beetle's life cycle and planning his planting to miss it, the farmer beat the potato beetle without having to fight it directly.

and borage to deter other insects; strawberries also like beans, onions, lettuce, and spinach, but dislike the cabbage family.

Sunflowers enjoy the company of cucumbers, but don't do well with pole beans or potatoes. **Sweet potatoes** like beans and lettuce, and white hellebore will control leaf-eating insects.

To keep **tomatoes** happy, plant them near asparagus, carrots, celery, chives, cucumbers, eggplant, lima beans, onions, parsley, and peppers. Basil nearby will improve tomato flavor and repel flies and mosquitoes. Both chives and mint improve tomato growth and flavor. Borage deters tomato hornworm, and marigolds repel nematodes. Avoid corn, dill, kohlrabi, and potatoes near tomatoes. **Turnips** like to be near peas, but dislike the cabbage family and kohlrabi. **Watermelons** get along with potatoes, but don't do well near tall vegetables.

Companion planting is a natural way to deter insects, and it imitates Nature's intended pattern of plant diversity. By filling your garden with mutually friendly plants, you can enhance growth and flavor, and repel harmful insects at the same time.

TIMED PLANTING

You can beat many of the most injurious pests simply by keeping their favorite food out of reach. If an insect's arrival coincides with your plants' most vulnerable stages, the damage can be devastating (to you and the plant). But if you have timed your planting to avoid that— by using your knowledge of insects' life cycles—the damage can be avoided. If there is no food for insects when they appear, they will not hang around, and they are much less likely to return.

Insect life cycles vary in different parts of the country. In the chilly north, an insect may manage only one generation per growing season. But in the warm south, that same species of insect can have several generations per season. Even different parts of the same state can show variations. That is why your garden notebook becomes so important. The details of when every species of insect actually arrived in your garden, when its leaf-munching little larvae started chomping on your plants, and when it left the area can guide your planting schedule.

TILLING AND MOWING

M any pests spend a part of their life cycle in the ground. By tilling at the right time, you can destroy them. Other pests overwinter in long grass, so by mowing it you get them, too. Some like to over-winter in crop residues left lying on the surface, and tilling before you plant a winter cover crop will kill them.

Fall tilling or plowing kills overwintering European corn borer, lar-vae of the wheat-stem sawfly, and cocoons of the grape berry moth. Fall or early spring tilling or plowing can expose grasshopper eggs to freezing or drying, or bury them so deeply that the nymphs cannot emerge after hatching. Summer tilling or disking destroys the white grubs of the Japanese beetle, white-fringed bee-tle, and the European chafer. Corn does better if the ground is plowed or tilled just before planting because this upsets the corn-root aphid and the ants that "herd" them. And by tilling in or plowing pea crops just after harvest, the life cycles of the pea weevil and grain cutworm are disrupted.

Tilling soil where insects lay eggs is an effective deterrent against their return.

Remember, however, that some beneficial insects also spend part of their life cycle as soil-dwellers, or overwinter in long grass. While you are killing harmful insects, you may also kill some beneficials. You must decide whether that sacrifice is worth it.

INSECT IDENTIFICATION

It is essential for gardeners to recognize the most common insects. We tend to glance at insects without really looking at them, but it's not hard to spot their distinguishing features. Once you can name 10 or 15 insects that you see every day in your garden and house, it becomes easier to recognize a new arrival. This is one of the many areas where the value of a written record—the garden note-book—becomes apparent.

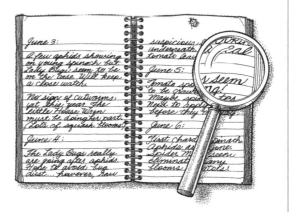

Starting in late winter or very early spring, note the arrival of insects. Record the species, date, and where the insect was seen. As spring gets under way you may note several "new" insects every day. Are they harmful, beneficial, or neutral? Are the harmful insects being hunted by predators or parasites? (If you find a weird insect that you cannot identify with this book or a field guide to insects, seek the help of your county Agricultural Cooperative Extension agent.) And when insects start to breed, which they will do very quickly, note that also.

It is very important that you keep your record up-to-date through the spring, summer, and fall. By the time winter rolls in you will have a dog-eared treasure, the life cycle of your garden's insects. It is a powerful tool that you will use consistently.

Once you know which insects arrive when, and what they do, you can plan the timing of next season's plantings to beat them. For example, you will be able to start your eggplants a month earlier so that they are big and strong enough to shrug off an attack by flea beetles. You will be able to get your squash, cucumbers, and melons well established and tucked under a protective floating-row cover well before squash bugs and cucumber beetles arrive. And you can time a beneficial insect order to deal with the depredations of a harmful insect population. Knowing what to expect, and when, helps prevent nasty surprises.

CATCHING AND PRESERVING INSECTS

You will undoubtedly come across many insects that you're unable to identify at first. In order to have time to consult reference books, or get the help of an entomologist or your county Cooperative Extension agent, you need a way to catch and preserve specimens. Putting them in an empty jar is good for an hour or so, but they will deteriorate soon after that.

Insect collecting is a fascinating hobby, but all you need is the basic essentials. You don't need a full panoply of entomology equipment.

Caterpillars and worms can be caught by hand, but legged and winged insects move too quickly for the finger-and-thumb approach. You can use a good quality child's butterfly net. For tiny insects, a moistened camel-hair brush works well because the insects will stick to the brush. Once caught, insects should be dropped immediately into the killing jar.

Isopropyl or ethyl alcohol will kill and preserve the insect for later identification.

To kill and preserve the insects, small glass jars with tight-fitting screw top metal lids filled three-quarters with ethyl alcohol or iso-propyl alcohol will do the job. Do not put more than one type of insect in a jar or identification may become difficult. Finally, a good magnifying glass, a pair of long, fine-pointed tweezers, and a piece of white plastic laminate, such as Formica, to put the specimens on, will complete your identification kit.

METAMORPHOSIS

Unlike animals, insects undergo their most important changes after emerging from the egg. Some insects hatch as a larva—a small caterpillar, worm, or maggot. The larva eats voraciously (destroying your weakest and most vulnerable plants in the process) until it's big enough to pupate. You can find pupae—small, plump, often shiny cylindrical brown cases or silken cocoons with one pointed and one rounded end—in garden litter or the crevices of trees. Inside the pupa casing, the insect metamorphoses into an adult that emerges full grown, often when weather warms up in spring.

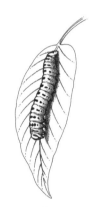

Insects have tremendous appetites in the larvae stage, but are susceptible to pest controls because of their soft skins.

Other insects have a simpler form of metamorphosis. They hatch as nymphs, or miniature adults. These nymphs, like larvae, eat huge quantities of food and grow amazingly fast. As they grow, they molt (shed their skins) several times, until they are full-grown adults. Their distant relatives, crabs and lobsters, do the same thing.

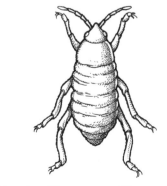

Nymphs will not pupate. They are born as immature versions of adult insects.

Larvae and nymphs have two things in common: they are not very mobile and are usually soft-skinned. This makes them an easy, tasty meal for any number of predators. Aphids, for example, can emerge as nymphs throughout the season, so several insects with shorter life cycles take advantage of this ever-present food source. This balances the scale: while aphids can be a constant threat to your plants, there is an almost endless procession of parasite and predator insects eager to control them for you. If your plants are strong and healthy, aphids will not do permanent damage before the predators arrive.

Attracting Beneficial Insects

Gardens attract insects no matter what you do. With the right precautions, harmful insects are discouraged. Careful interplanting of target and repellent plants, ingenious traps, and other measures are all effective. Best of all, however, is when bad bugs are eaten by predatory insects called beneficials.

We can, of course, let Nature take her course and hope that the right predators, parasites, and pollinators arrive in time to save our precious plants. But as organic gardeners, we can help Nature along without disturbing the balance we seek. There are two ways to do this: grow plants that attract beneficials (and create an environment where they will stay around), or buy them to release in our gardens.

It almost goes without saying that chemical pesticides must be avoided at all costs. They kill beneficial, neutral, and harmful insects with the same deadly efficiency, and poison the environment to boot. To attract beneficials you should grow a diversity of plants such as alyssum, yarrow, bee balm, and angelica, and even let some of your vegetables run to seed. Herbs produce small flowers that attract a wide range of helpful insects, as do many cover crops. Many beneficials are themselves quite tiny, and they like to feed on the nectar and pollen of small flowers. These plants also provide shade in hot, dry regions. If you encourage beneficials in the fall and can provide winter shelter, such as a hedgerow of perennial shrubs, many of them will be around in the spring when you need them.

BUYING BENEFICIAL INSECTS

There may come a time when you're faced with a sudden infestation of damaging insects. If you can get beneficial insects delivered in time, which is critical, they'll probably do a good job for you. Unless you can persuade them to stay, however, they will then almost certainly leave for richer pastures, insectwise, leaving your garden vulnerable to the next wave of attackers. If your garden has been planned to appeal to beneficials, however, enough may stay around to help out should another infestation threaten your garden.

Insectaries (businesses that grow insects) are doing a booming business in dozens of beneficial insects and are often quite responsive to customers in dire need. Help will arrive in a sealed packet containing several thousand insects. Most come with release instructions: weather conditions, time of day, and so on. Some soil-living beneficials, such as nematodes, have to be mixed with water and poured on the garden. If conditions for their release are not optimum, follow the instructions for temporary storage, or call the supplier for advice. It is disappointing to release 5,000 ladybugs in the afternoon and find them all gone the next day.

THE POLLINATORS

Many plants depend on insects to help with the pollination process. Without them, these plants would be unable to reproduce. For example, the squash bee pollinates pumpkins, squash, and other members of the gourd family. If these plants are not pollinated by helpful insects, they won't yield any fruit. Apples, pears, plums, and sweet cherries can only form fruit when insects carry pollen from flowers on one tree to flowers on another.

Plants have developed flowers designed to attract pollinators such as bees, flies, and other bugs. Flower color and the scent of nectar are the initial attractions, but it is impossible for insects to reach the sweet nectar without getting some pollen on their bodies. As an insect wriggles and pushes into a flower to get at the nectar, its body is showered with pollen. When the insect visits another plant, some of that pollen is deposited in the next flower, causing cross-pollination. The furry bodies of bees are well suited to this task and their methodical behavior assures pollination of a range of plants.

Including domestic honeybees, bees are responsible for most pollination. There are about 5,000 species of wild bees in the United States. Pollination is done mostly by solitary bees, often known as mason bees because many species use mud and pebbles to construct their nests. The orchard mason, or blue orchard bee, is an iridescent blue; it will indiscriminately pollinate all kinds of fruit trees except citrus. In warm, humid parts of the country the horn-faced bee also pollinates fruit trees; they are 80 percent more efficient at pollination than honeybees. The alfalfa leafcutting bee originated in Asia, but this small blackish-brown bee now lives in woodlands all across America, pollinating alfalfa, cucumbers, and clover.

Solitary bees are better pollinators than honeybees because they will fly in cool, damp weather when honeybees tend to stay at home in their hives. The bumblebee, although not technically a solitary bee, is equally important in its visits to tomatoes, peppers, eggplant, cucumbers, melons, blueberries, and many other crops.

Flies are the next most important group of pollinators. Metallic blue-green blowflies pollinate vegetable crops, including carrots, onions, Brussels sprouts, kale, and cabbage. Many species of wasp are important pollinators; in fact, the only insect known to pollinate fig trees is the fig wasp. Some butterflies and moths act as pollinators, too, including hawk and sphinx moths, and swallowtail, painted lady, monarch, and brush-footed butterflies. Hummingbirds are also excellent pollinators but their population is radically lower than their insect counterparts.

You can encourage pollinators in your garden by allowing some of your property to grow wild, where bees and other pollinating insects can forage and nest. Plant flowers to feed them in and around your vegetable garden. To attract wild bees, bore 10 or 15 holes in 6-inch-deep logs or blocks of wood. Vary the size of the holes—⅛, ¼, and ⅜ inch. Place the blocks in sheltered spots all around your yard at different heights, from ground level to 6 feet. And don't worry about getting stung—most of these bees do not sting!

BENEFICIAL INSECTS

This list will help you recognize dozens of insects that should be welcomed into your garden. Some occur naturally and may appear in the nick of time to deal with an infestation of harmful insects. Others may have to be purchased quickly when you need to help Mother Nature along a bit. Suppliers can be found in Resources at the end of this book.

Ant lions resemble tiny dragonflies, are dark brown, and have a yellow marking behind their heads. The brown or gray larva is known as the doodlebug. They hunt by building cone-shaped pits in sandy soil that ants fall into. It is amusing to watch them build these pits: they walk backward in decreasing circles, shoveling out soil with a flip of their heads.

The **aphid midge** is a tiny ($\frac{1}{16}$-inch) nocturnal fly. Its larva is a bright orange maggot that attacks more than 60 species of aphids found on vegetables, flowers, shrubs, and trees. The eggs are tiny orange ovals, laid at night, that hatch in two to four days. The last generation in fall will overwinter in the soil, emerging in the spring. They are attracted to  dill, mustard, thyme, sweet clover, and other pollen and nectar plants. They are sold commercially.

Aphid parasites are tiny black or brown bugs related to the braconid wasp. They feed on several aphids, including green peach, melon, and pea aphids. The larvae are tiny white grubs that develop inside the host pest's body.

Assassin bugs are flat $\frac{3}{4}$-inch-long insects with long, narrow heads and curving beaks. Some species squeak! They are often brightly colored, although some disguise themselves with dust or garden litter. They feed on flies, tomato hornworms, and other large caterpillars. The nymphs hibernate and emerge in June.

Big-eyed bugs are noted for their bulging eyes and big appetites. They are $\frac{1}{8}$- to $\frac{1}{4}$-inch long, gray, brown, black, or tan with tiny black spots, and are easily confused with the harmful tarnished plant bug.

Their diet includes the eggs and small larvae of aphids, small caterpillars and worms, spider mites, leafhoppers, flea beetles, mealybugs, and thrips. Adults will remain active until fall as long as there is a cover crop. They hibernate in garden litter, emerging in spring to lay eggs on plant stems and the undersides of leaves. They are attracted to alfalfa, potatoes, beets, and clover.

Braconid wasps are tiny, wasp-waisted, black or brown, ¹⁄₁₀- to ½-inch-long parasitic wasps that inject their eggs into host insects. Some adults paralyze the host insect first. The eggs hatch, then the larvae kill and consume the host. Although they are wasps, they cannot sting humans. If you see a caterpillar studded with what looks like small grains of rice, it has been parasited by the braconid wasp. Even if it's a harmful cater-

pillar, let it live! The larvae will soon kill it, and they will reproduce to provide continued protection for your garden. They also prey on aphids, beetle larvae, and many other insects. Braconids are attracted to nectar plants with small flowers, such as parsley, wild carrot, mustard, lemon balm, stinging nettle, and yarrow. They are sold commercially.

The **chalcid wasp** is *very* tiny, ¹⁄₁₀₀- to ¹⁄₃₂-inch long, usually yellow with dark markings or metallic black. It is a member of the trichogramma family. Chalcids attack pest eggs, larvae, and pupae, and are considered important parasitic beneficials. Their larvae destroy scales, mealybugs, thrips, cabbage butterflies, and aphids, plus various moths and beetles. Some species attack the Mexican bean beetle and the greenhouse whitefly. They are attracted to pollen and nectar plants, and will shelter under tall plants such as sunflowers. The golden chalcid is sold commercially.

Damsel bugs are long, slender, gray or brown insects that dart around on long legs. Their eggs are laid in plant tissue and hatch in about a week. The nymphs eat aphids, leafhoppers, thrips, and a variety of caterpillars, many of which are much larger than they are. Adults will overwinter. They are attracted to alfalfa.

Dragonflies benefit the gardener more than the garden. They consume thousands of mosquitoes, flies, and midges. They catch their prey in midair by curling their legs to form a scoop basket that can hold as many as 100 mosquitoes. A dragonfly can eat its weight in mosquitoes in half an hour. By the way, dragonflies do *not* bite people or horses. You can attract them into your garden with long upright stakes higher than the plant foliage; they will perch on top and scan the area for prey.

Fireflies (sometimes called lightning bugs) are soft-bodied brown or black insects. Their larvae eat many garden pests, including slugs, snails, cutworms, and other insect larvae. Some adults appear to eat nothing at all. The flashes you see are mostly from adult males seeking mates. The wingless females lay their eggs on the ground (in some species they become luminous as the larvae develop) and they hatch in about a month. The larvae are successful at controlling slugs in perennial plantings. Fireflies congregate around trees and moist areas. The best ways to encourage them is to preserve their natural environment.

Ground beetles are large (¾- to 1-inch) and leggy blue-black or brown beetles, usually with an iri-descent sheen. They are nocturnal and hide under stones by day. More than 2,500 species of ground beetle are found in the United States. They feed on snails, slugs, cutworms, Colorado potato beetle larvae, and tree insects such as gypsy moths and tent caterpillars. You can collect them from rotting trees.

Ichneumon wasps prey on caterpillars and beetle larvae. Some are tiny, only ¹⁄₁₀-inch long, while other species are as much as 1½-inches long. The females inject their eggs into their prey, using a long ovipositor that looks like (but is not) a stinger. Their larvae are white, tapered grubs. Ichneumon wasps are an important native parasite of harmful insects. They like 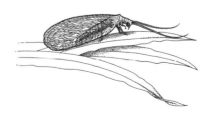pollen and nectar plants, fava beans, and vetch. You can give them a thank-you treat by letting some broccoli plants and radishes flower.

Lacewings are fragile, slender, green or brown, and ½- to ¾-inch long, with large eyes and large diaphanous wings. The larvae are mottled yellow to brown, with spines visible along their sides. They destroy soft-bodied insects of all kinds, including aphids, thrips, mealybugs, some scales, moth eggs, small caterpillars, and mites. They are attracted to nectar and pollen plants such as angelica, corn, goldenrod, and dandelion.

The **ladybug**, also known as the lady beetle and ladybird beetle, is perhaps the best-known beneficial insect. Adults are ¹⁄₁₆- to ⅜-inch long,

  pale yellow to dark reddish-orange, and some have black spots. Other members of this family are all black, or black with red spots. Larvae are ferocious eaters. They resemble tiny alligators, with bumpy gray or black bodies and orange, yellow, or pink markings. Adults and larvae consume huge quantities of aphids, mealybugs, scales, mites, and insect eggs. They are attracted to pollen- and nectar-producing flowers such as angelica and dill, and to growing grains. Their egg clusters are yellow or white ovals laid upright on the undersides of leaves. Purchased adults may disappear overnight, so buying larvae is a better bet.

The **mealybug destroyer** is aptly named. The adult is a ⅓-inch oval beetle with black wing-covers and a coral head. The larvae are

 creamy white, with segmented bodies and long waxy hairs; they can be mistaken for mealybugs, so look closely before you run for the spray bottle. Females lay their eggs among mealybug egg masses. The eggs hatch in 10 days, and the larvae (and adults) feed voraciously on mealybug eggs and larvae. If you have a mealybug infestation on houseplants or in a greenhouse, you can release some destroyers on the plant and cover it with row-cover material to confine them. They are sold commercially.

Minute pirate bugs will eat just about anything, but prefer thrips, spider mites, the eggs of many insects, small caterpillars, leafhopper

nymphs, and corn earworms. The adults are black and white, with a pattern of three black triangles on their backs. The nymphs are shiny wingless insects that change color from yellow to orange to brown as they grow. Eggs are laid on alfalfa stems, green clover leaves and petals, and corn silks. The voracious nymphs hatch within five days. They are attracted to alfalfa, goldenrod, daisies, yarrow, corn, stinging nettles, clover, willows, and other shrubs. Adults will overwinter in crevices and garden litter.

Paper wasps are a mixed blessing. These black or brown wasps have yellow or light-colored markings. Fertilized females overwinter in crevices and buildings and chew wood into pulp to build their familiar gray nests. They prey on many types of caterpillars, including hornworms, cabbageworms, and gypsy moths. Nevertheless, they are related to yellow jackets and hornets, and although they are more passive than their unfriendly relatives, they will sting if they feel their nest is being threatened.

The **praying mantis** (or mantid) is a famous predator with a well-deserved reputation. They are large insects, up to 4 inches long, usually green and brown, that perch on a twig with their enlarged forelegs held poised for attack. Adult mantises will eat anything they can catch, from aphids to small frogs and salamanders, even 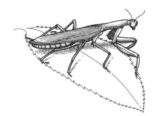 other mantises. The eggs are laid on stems and twigs in a frothy mass that hardens into a papery case. You can collect egg cases to import into your garden. Do not detach the case, just cut the whole stem to which it is anchored. Store it in a paper bag in the refrigerator. (Do not store the egg cases in a warm room, or they will hatch and your room will soon be filled with tiny mantises!) In early spring, tie the stem to a 3-foot cane or stake in the garden. Several hundred praying mantis nymphs will emerge. Egg cases are sold commercially, but it's better to collect them locally.

Not all mites are harmful. **Predatory mites** prey on spider mites, two-spotted mites, red mites, and Pacific mites. They lay eggs among spider mite webs, and the nymphs hatch in two days. You are unlikely to find predatory mites in the wild, so if you need them to control

an infestation of red mites on roses, for example, you will have to purchase them.

   Predatory thrips are very small. Under a magnifying glass, you will
see that they are yellow with black spots on their wings. They prey on

the eggs and larvae of spider mites,
aphids, thrips, Oriental fruit moths,
codling moths, bud moths, peach
tree borers, alfalfa weevils, whiteflies, leaf miner flies, and scales.
Predatory thrips lay their eggs in
leaves and stems and will eat plant
juices and pollen; however, this does little damage.

   The **robber fly** will capture many flying insects, including horse-
flies, leafhoppers, grasshoppers, beetles, and other flies. These big, powerful flies buzz like a bee in flight, so they are sometimes written off as a
buzz-fly and swatted if they fly into the house. They have hairy bodies,
often gray or black with yellow markings. The larvae are particularly
valuable, as they live in the soil and eat grubs and grasshopper eggs.

   Rove beetles are slender, brown or black, ⅒- to 1-inch long, and
look like a slightly plump earwig. They feed on aphids, springtails, nematodes, fly eggs, and maggots in the soil. Some will attack cabbage-root
maggots and fly larvae. When disturbed, a rove beetle will respond by curling the tip of its abdomen over its back. You can encourage this beneficial
by planting strips of rye or other grains as a cover crop, mulching plant
beds, and using stone or plank walkways under which they can hide.

   Spined soldier bugs are shield-shaped, ½-inch long, brown or yellow, and covered with black specks. They have sharp points on their
shoulders. The nymphs are wingless miniatures of the adults. Eggs are a
metallic bronze, laid on leaves in clusters of about twelve. Attracted to
permanent plantings of perennials, adults and nymphs feed on the very
destructive fall armyworm, the larvae of Colorado potato beetle and
Mexican bean beetle, and tent caterpillars. They are sold commercially.

   The **syrphid** family includes hover flies and flower flies. These tiny,
brightly colored flies literally hover; their wings move so fast they appear invisible. Larvae are gray or green, with pointed heads, and look rather slug-

like. Adults live on pollen and nectar (they are extremely efficient pollinators) while the voracious larvae can quickly control an infestation. Adults are attracted to pollen and nectar flowers such as marigolds, parsley, wild carrots, and yarrow.

Tachinid flies look like burly, overgrown houseflies. They are gray, brown, or black, ⅓- to ½-inch long, and often covered in bristles. Eggs are laid on or near host species, which die when the larvae (maggots) hatch. They attack cutworms, armyworms, tent caterpillars, cabbage loopers, gypsy moths, Japanese beetles, May beetles, squash beetles, green stinkbugs, and sow 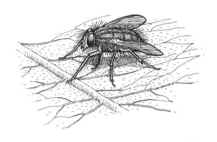 bugs. Tachinids are attracted to pollen and nectar flowers, including dill, sweet clover, wild carrot, goldenrod, amaranth, and various herbs.

Tiger beetle adults are long-legged, ½- to ¾-inch long, and can run very fast. They are often brightly colored in metallic blue, black, green, or red. Both adults and larvae prey on insects of many kinds, but mainly pest species. Females lay a single egg in a soil burrow; it takes up to three years for the larvae to develop to adulthood; larvae feed on insects that fall into the burrow.

Trichogramma wasps are tiny yellow creatures with dark abdomens and red eyes. The larvae are minute white grubs that live in host insects. The female wasp lays her eggs inside the host insect's eggs. They prey on more than 200 species of moths, including spring budworms, cotton bullworms, tomato hornworms, corn earworms, corn borers, and codling moths. You  can encourage trichogramma wasps to a diverse planting of dill, anise, and caraway; in orchards, provide a mixture of clover and flowering weeds to attract them. They are sold commercially.

The **whitefly parasite** is a tiny, parasitic wasp. It has a black thorax and a yellow abdomen. Females lay their eggs inside immature whiteflies, which turn black as the larvae pupate inside them. In moderate conditions, the life cycle takes about three weeks. Whitefly parasites are not native, so you must purchase them. They are most successful against greenhouse whiteflies, but in warm sunny conditions, they can be effective in gardens. Release two to five parasites per tomato or squash plant when whiteflies first appear, then repeat in two weeks. They may overwinter in mild areas.

Western predatory mites are fast-moving, reddish-tan mites native to the United States. They feast on spider mites, especially the European red mite and the citrus red mite. The female lays her eggs among spider mites; the nymphs hatch in three to four days and become adults a day later. The adults overwinter in the cracks and crevices of tree bark. They are attracted to pollen plants. Release 50 to 100 mites per apple tree in summer or early fall to establish a permanent population. For serious infestations, release 1,000 per tree. They are sold commercially.

SPIDERS

O ne of the best insect predators in a garden is not an insect. Spiders are members of the arachnid family. Insects have six legs, spiders have eight. Dozens of varieties can be found in a chemical-free garden, and with only two exceptions (see page 45), they are all beneficial. Spiders hunt continuously. Some stalk and attack their prey, others spin webs

and wait patiently for an insect to blunder into them. They are deterrents as well as predators. Most insects will rapidly leave the area if they sense a spider nearby. Unlike some beneficial insects, spiders will not desert your garden for lack of prey. And they will eat just about anything they can catch, from aphids to beetles; 80 percent of their diet is harmful insects. Mulch, compost piles, and overwinter cover crops attract spiders. But you must avoid chemicals or pesticides because spiders are particularly vulnerable to them.

To most people, all spiders are alike. But organic gardeners should know that there are nine families of garden spiders that are ready and

SPIDERS THAT BITE

Only two garden spiders can bite humans: the black widow and the brown recluse. Both will try to avoid you, but they will bite if they feel threatened (which doesn't take much). If you are bitten by either one, seek medical attention *immediately*. If you develop an allergic reaction to the bite—5 percent of the population is allergic to various bites and stings—it can become a medical emergency.

Female black widows have a red hourglass design on the abdomen. They are found in dark places, under sticks, rocks, trash, and even garden furniture. Male black widows rarely bite. The brown recluse is tan with a distinct violin-shaped black mark on the front section of the body. Favorite hiding places are garden sheds, garages, and woodpiles.

You will probably feel a black widow bite, whereas you might not notice a brown recluse bite. In either case, the bite can result in redness, swelling, and a small blister at the site of the bite. Without medical treatment, you may develop nausea, stomach cramps, and profuse sweating. For some people this can become a life-threatening emergency. Have someone take you to the emergency room immediately (do not attempt to drive yourself), or call an ambulance.

eager to eat your insect pests. Even if you don't like spiders for some reason, it's advantageous to have them in your garden.

Orb weaver spiders (at left) spin sticky webs on and between plants. Many spin a new web every dawn or dusk, then wait in the center of the web for their prey. Some orb weavers spin a zigzag pattern in the center of their webs. They vary in size and color, but will feast on many nasty bugs, including the carrot rust fly. The larger members of this family will even eat hard-bodied insects such as grasshoppers and beetles.

Sheet-web weavers spin a flat, almost horizontal web. They hang upside down beneath the web until a prey insect lands in it. Then they pull the insect down through the web. These small brown or black spiders eat aphids, grasshoppers, springtails, and other soft-bodied insects. Brown, gray, or green mesh-web weavers spin fuzzy webs in crevices in tree bark, beneath leaves, and on the tips of plant stems. Their diet includes stinkbugs.

Combfooted spiders have comblike bristles on their hind legs, which they use to fling silken strands over their prey. Usually light in color, these spiders have a noticeably large abdomen. They spin irregular webs in fences, among rocks, and between the low branches of trees and shrubs. The American house spider and the infamous black widow are members of this family.

Funnel-web weavers create a web with a funnel-shaped section in

which they hide. When prey lands in the web, they rush out and secure it before dragging it back into the funnel. They vary in color from pale yellow with gray markings to reddish-brown with black markings. Funnel-web weavers can be found in leaf litter, stone fences, low shrubs, and grassy areas.

Wolf spiders are night hunters. They spin no webs, hiding during the day and coming out at night to stalk aphids, leafhoppers, grasshoppers, and beetles. Some are quite large—up to 1½-inches long—and if you visit your garden at night with a flashlight, you may see the pink or green reflection of their eyes.

Jumping spiders can make impressive leaps to capture their prey. They are not web builders, although they may release a silken dragline as they leap. With the sharpest vision of all spiders, they eat a range of insects from cockroaches to spotted cucumber beetles. They are green, red, or gray, with red, white, and black markings.

Lynx spiders are found on plants, tall grasses, and shrubs. Like jumping spiders, they spin no web but may release a dragline as they seize their prey. Their diet includes fire ants, tarnished plant bugs, and cotton fleahoppers. When hunting, many lynx spiders sit back on their hind legs with their front legs raised, ready to pounce. They are green, tan, or gray.

Crab spiders are easily recognized: they hold their legs stretched out to the side, and can move forward, sideways, or backward. They wait on the ground, in flowers, or on plants for their prey of carrot rust fly or Colorado potato beetle. They are often the same color as the flowers they frequent.

The well-known **daddy longlegs** (also known as harvestmen) are not spiders, although they are a member of the arachnid family. They eat aphids, snails, earthworms, flies, spiders, and even other daddy longlegs. They are harmless to humans and pets. Largely nocturnal, they prefer cool, sheltered areas and need moisture to survive.

HARMFUL INSECTS

The alphabetically ordered entries that follow contain the insect's general description, identifying characteristic, information about its life cycle, and brief hints on control methods. There are several good field guides to insects available at your library and local bookstore if you want more information. Don't be discouraged by the size of this list. You will see only a few of these harmful insects in your garden, depending on what you grow and where you live. If your plants are healthy, the damage will be minimal.

Aphid: These small, soft-bodied insects are shaped like pears and come in a variety of colors, including brown, green, gray, rosy red, gold, and black. They are usually wingless, but if a colony becomes overcrowded, winged females are born to migrate to other plants. Aphids have two tubelike protrusions called cornicles on their rear end, which are used to suck out nourishment from your plants. Aphids excrete a sweet liquid called honeydew; ants feed on this and will herd aphids just like cattle to control this food source. Aphids attack almost every plant and fruit tree. Symptoms include curled yellow leaves, stunted shoots, and seedling death. They can also transmit viruses. A female aphid bears up

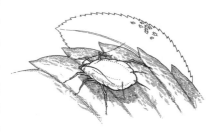

to 100 live young a week during the growing season. One generation overwinters as eggs. Aphids can appear at any time. *Control:* A strong blast of water will wash them off plants, or you can crush them with your fingers. Spray insecticidal soap. Spray superfine oils in summer (such as Oil-Away) on vegetables, flowers, and roses. Horticultural oils kill overwintering eggs on dormant fruit trees. Many beneficial insects, including green lacewings and ladybugs, eat aphids.

Asiatic garden beetle: Chestnut-brown and about ¾-inch long, they emerge in late summer to lay eggs in soil. White soil-dwelling grubs feed on young roots, favoring poorly nourished grass and strawberry patches. Adults feed on butterfly bush, roses, chrysanthemums, dahlias, and goldenrod; in the vegetable garden they eat the foliage of carrots, beets, eggplant, peppers, and turnips, and will attack peach and cherry trees. Mainly nocturnal, they are attracted to lights and can be found on window screens and around porch or deck lights. As the weather turns cooler, larvae burrow deep into the soil, resurfacing to pupate in late spring. *Control:* Beneficial nematodes eat larvae. Dry conditions help kill eggs and young larvae. Insecticidal soap is effective against adult beetles.

Asparagus beetle: The wing-covers bear a black cross and four black dots on a white ground, and a reddish-brown border. Adults about ¼-inch long emerge from hibernation and lay eggs on early asparagus spears; these are visible as small shiny black spots. Larvae and adults chew on spears and foliage. Eggs hatch in seven days. Larvae feed for two to three weeks, then pupate in the soil, emerging as adults in 10 to 14 days. Adults overwinter in garden trash and on dead asparagus fronds. *Control:* Handpick and destroy adults, larvae, and eggs. Pollen and nectar plants attract predatory and parasitic insects. Spray Bt or superfine horticultural oil.

Azalea lace bug: This brownish-gray insect is about ⅛-inch long and has lacy wings. The female lays hundreds of eggs, which look like light oval spots surrounded by a dark reddish discoloration. The eggs hatch around the beginning of May in the mid-Atlantic states, earlier in the south, later in the north. Nymphs shed their skin five times in two weeks to become adults. One generation overwinters as eggs. These bugs love azaleas, both native deciduous types and Asian evergreens. Symptoms of attack include tiny white stipple marks on the upper surfaces of leaves and black spots of fecal matter on the undersides of leaves. In severe infestations, leaves become almost white and drop off. *Control:* Spray undersides of leaves in early spring with insecticidal soap or superfine horticultural oil.

Black vine weevil: These are brown or black ⅓-inch weevils. The larvae are pinkish-white with brown heads and overwinter in the soil. They emerge in June as adults to lay eggs in the soil. Larvae damage plant roots of evergreens, grapes, strawberries, and small fruits, often killing the plant. Adult damage to leaf edges is usually cosmetic and doesn't threaten the plant. *Control:* Hunt them at night with a flashlight. Handpick adults at dusk. Release beneficial nematodes to kill soil-dwelling grubs. Try a foliar spray containing Beauvaria bassiana, a natural fungus that kills adults. Bands of tape wrapped around trunks and coated with a sticky substance prevent adults from reaching foliage.

Blister beetle: These insects, about ¾-inch long, have long legs, long bodies, and narrow necks and heads. They can be black, blue, purple, green, or brown. The striped blister beetle is greenish-yellow with black stripes. Feeding on flowers and leaves of vegetables and flowers, adults can totally defoliate a plant. Larvae overwinter in a legless, thick-skinned stage and pupate in spring, emerging as adults in early summer. The larvae 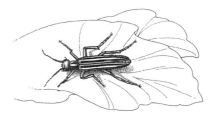 are beneficial, since they feed on grasshopper eggs. Blister beetles contain cantharidin, which can cause blisters on your skin. They can be very toxic to horses if consumed among alfalfa hay. *Control:* Knock beetles into a jar or bucket containing rubbing alcohol or detergent water; be sure to wear rubber or other tough gloves and protective clothing. Dust plants with rotenone or spray with pyrethrin.

Cabbage looper: Mottled gray moths are marked with a silver spot on each wing. Their wingspan is 1½ to 2 inches. Larvae are green caterpillars with a white line down each side. They move by looping their bodies into a hump. Adults emerge in May to lay eggs. Larvae feed for up to a month, then pupate in cocoons. Up to four generations a year are hatched. Larvae attack brassica family crops and other vegetables, including spinach, potatoes, tomatoes, and lettuce. *Control:* Protect plants with floating row covers. Spray with Bt, or release trichogramma wasps for large infestations.

Cabbage-root fly: This insect attacks all members of the brassica family: cabbage, broccoli, cauliflower, Brussels sprout, mustard, kale, arugula, cress, turnip, and radish. The gray and black adult resembles an ordinary housefly and deposits its eggs on soil near the base of plants. The maggots pupate after three weeks and emerge as adults two weeks later. Emergence peaks in the spring. Symptoms include wilting plants, bacterial or fungal diseases, irregular holes along leaf edges, and tiny pebbles of dark green frass. Larvae hide along leaf veins and in the crevices between leaves. *Control:* Use row covers in early spring; radishes can be left covered for the entire season.

Cabbageworm: The adult is the well-known white cabbage butterfly, which has white or pale yellow wings with three or four black spots. Yellow bullet-shaped eggs are laid at the base of leaves and hatch in five days. Larvae are small, bright green, smooth caterpillars that can be hard to spot since they exactly match the color of the leaf on which they are feeding. They deposit small piles of dark green frass on leaves. All mem-

bers of the brassica family are attacked: cabbage, broccoli, cauliflower, Brussels sprout, kale, mustard, turnip, arugula, cress, and radish. Larvae eat large ragged holes in leaves and will tunnel into heads of cabbage. *Control:* Keep crops under row covers. Spray Bt when butterflies are first seen. Continue spraying weekly until butterflies are gone. Rotate your plants to a new location next year.

Carrot rust fly: Adults are metallic greenish-black, about ¼-inch long, with a yellow head and legs. They emerge in April or May to lay eggs on young carrots at the soil line. Larvae feed on root hairs first, then burrow into the root, causing extensive damage and stunting or killing the plant. In addition to carrots, they sometimes attack parsnips, celery, and dill. Depending on climate and weather conditions, they may produce two or three generations a season. *Control:* Sow carrot seed after the first generation emerges, and harvest it within a month of when the second generation starts laying eggs. Use floating row covers.

Chinch bug: It is a black bug, ¹⁄₁₆-inch long, with white wings bearing a small triangular dot. Young nymphs are red with a white stripe. Adults overwinter in grass roots and emerge in spring to lay eggs on grass roots in warm, sunny locations. Nymphs feed on corn leaves and stalks and grass roots, destroying large patches of lawn grass or pasture. Two or three generations a year are possible. *Control:* Turn up a band of soil around corn and apply creosote. On turf grass, soak the area with soapy water, then cover it with old blankets; bugs will emerge and can be scooped up with the blanket. Wash them out and kill them with very hot, soapy water.

Codling moth: This insect loves apples, but will feed on other fruits, nuts, and leaves. Adults are a mottled gray-brown with dark brown wing tips and a ¾-inch wingspan. Larvae are pinkish-white caterpillars, ¾- to 1-inch long. Larvae eat leaves, then burrow into fruit and feed for a few weeks, emerging to pupate under loose bark or in the ground beneath trees. They can produce two or three generations a year. *Control:* Cleanliness is the best prevention: remove loose bark, clean up fallen fruit and leaves, and maintain a circle of bare earth around the trunk. Spray with superfine horti-

cultural oil before buds open to kill the eggs. Release trichogramma minutum wasps at two-week intervals. Fruit can be protected with paper bags tied around the stem. Spray Bt when the eggs start to hatch and repeat weekly.

Colorado potato beetle: Adults and larvae feed on the leaves of potato, tomato, eggplant, and pepper plants; they also like petunias. Adults, about ⅓-inch long, are yellow with 10 lengthwise black stripes and a reddish thorax and head with black spots. Larvae are dark orange, fat grubs, ¹⁄₁₆- to ½-inch long, with a double row of black spots on each side. Eggs are

shiny orange ovals laid on end in clusters on the undersides of leaves. Females will lay 1,000 eggs over several months. The larvae feed for two to three weeks, then pupate in the soil; they emerge as adults 5 to 10 days later. There may be two or three generations per season. One generation overwinters in the soil, emerging in the spring. *Control:* Mulch seedlings 2 to 3 inches deep with clean straw when they first emerge. Spray Bt *san diego* or M-Trak when larvae appear and repeat spraying weekly. Spray with rotenone or liquid rotenone/pyrethrin mix. Release purchased ladybugs. Douse the soil with beneficial nematodes to kill larvae.

Corn earworm: These rust-colored moths have a 1½- to 2-inch wingspan. Eggs are laid on leaves and corn silks. The 1- to 2-inch-long caterpillar larvae feed on corn, lettuce, peas, beans, tomatoes, squash, and potatoes. Larvae feed for two to four weeks, then pupate in the soil. There can be from one to seven generations a year. They overwinter in the soil as pupae. *Control:* In northern areas, avoid damage by planting early. Spray Bt when worms are first seen and repeat weekly. Three to seven days after corn silks appear, apply 20 drops of mineral oil with an eyedropper to corn silk just inside each ear; this suffocates worms and doesn't affect corn flavor. Corn varieties such as Country Gentleman and Silver Cross Bantam have long, tight husks that help prevent earworms from penetrating.

Cucumber beetle: This insect comes in two varieties, spotted and striped. Both are about ¼-inch long. The spotted type is sometimes mistaken for the lady beetle; it is yellowish-green with 11 or 12 black spots. Overwintering adults emerge in spring. Eggs are laid in the soil at the base of plants. The larvae are ½-inch white grubs with brown patches that feed for two to four weeks before pupating. Depending on the climate, they produce from one to three generations per season. They feed on corn roots, killing young plants and crippling older ones, and on squash family leaves and flowers, other vegetable crops, and annual and perennial flowers. They can spread bacterial wilt and cucumber mosaic virus. The striped cucumber beetle is

yellowish-orange with three black stripes. Adults emerge in spring, laying eggs in the soil near the base of plants. Eggs hatch in 10 days. Larvae are small white grubs that live in the soil eating roots for two to six weeks before pupating. They emerge as adults two weeks later to feed on flowers and fruit of squash family plants, peas, beans, corn, and many annual and perennial flowers. As they feed they spread wilt and mosaic virus diseases. *Control:* Plant late after beetles have laid eggs. Protect plants with floating row covers. Spray adult beetles with insecticidal soap mixed with pyrethrin. Apply beneficial nematodes to soil to kill larvae. Plant marigolds and radishes as deterrents. Heavy mulches are recommended.

Cutworm: These brown or gray nocturnal moths have a wingspan of about 1½ inches. Winds blow these moths north each spring, while later generations are blown south by cold fronts. Eggs are laid on soil or in grass from early May to early June. After feeding for three to five weeks, the larvae pupate in the soil, emerging in late August through September. Some species overwinter as eggs, others as pupae. Larvae of most species are fat gray-brown caterpillars up to 2 inches long. The army cutworm is darker, with a smart white stripe down its back. After feeding, they burrow into the soil near the base of the destroyed plant. They favor seedlings and young transplants, which are sev-

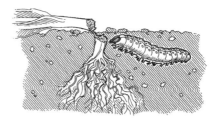

ered at the base or completely consumed. *Control:* Remove weeds and plant debris from your garden before planting to starve larvae. Release beneficial nematodes to kill larvae in the soil. Release trichogramma wasps to parasitize larvae. Mix Bt *kurstaki* with bran and molasses and sprinkle on soil before planting to kill larvae. Protect stems with cardboard or metal collars pressed into the soil. If you find a plant that's been attacked by a cutworm, look in the top couple of inches of soil near the base of the plant; you will find the culprit curled up, sleeping off its meal.

Diamondback moth: These slender, brown, ½-inch-long insects have long, pale antennae and a diamond pattern visible on their folded wings; the wings flare upward at the tips. The larva is pale green with a brown head and a distinctive V on the rear end. Adults overwinter to lay eggs on the leaves of host plants in spring. Larvae chew holes in leaves and burrow into heads of cabbage, broccoli, and cauliflower. From egg to larvae to adult takes about a month, so up to six generations a year are possible. *Control:* Plant resistant varieties such as michihli Chinese cabbage, mammoth red rock cabbage, and purple top white globe turnips. Apply Bt as soon as larvae damage appears on leaves.

Earwig: These slender, brown, ¾- to 1-inch-long insects have distinctive rear pincers (which, by the way, cannot bite humans). They are nocturnal feeders. The earwig is half good, half bad. It scavenges on decaying matter and is a predator of insect larvae, snails, and several other

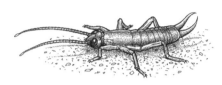

slow-moving insects. However, it can also overrun your garden, attacking fragile young transplants of vegetables and flowers. They are said not to like tomatoes, but they will eat potatoes, peppers, zinnias, dahlias, and roses—particularly the flowers. *Control:* Earwigs are a communal bunch, hiding during the day in moist, dark places. They can be trapped in bamboo sections or pieces of corrugated cardboard laid flat on the ground and emptied every morning into a bucket of detergent water.

European corn borer: This yellowish-brown nocturnal moth has two darker brown serrated lines along the wing tips; the wingspan is about 1 inch. Cream-colored egg masses are laid on the undersides of corn leaves.

Larvae are pinkish, with small dark brown spots on each segment. Fully grown larvae overwinter in corn stalks, then pupate and emerge as moths in June. There can be up to four generations a year. Larvae do serious damage to corn, pepper, potato, and bean crops, often boring into corn ears or plant stems and crippling or killing the plant. *Control:* Find entrance holes and remove the borers by hand. Apply Bt *kurstaki* bait to whorls while insects are feeding. Spray with rotenone or a garlic spray. Remove and destroy corn stalks after harvest.

Fall armyworm: This mottled gray-brown moth has light markings. A mature larva has a prominent inverted Y on its head. Eggs are laid in masses up to 100 and take only three days to hatch. Larvae are nocturnal and eat tender plants for about 12 days, then pupate in the soil for another 12 days. Adults emerge, mate on their second night, and lay eggs the next day. The armyworm attacks corn, grasses, cabbage, cotton, tobacco, and peanuts. *Control:* Grow early corn varieties that mature before armyworms arrive—July in the south, August in the north.

Fire ant: The bites of these ants can be deadly if you are allergic to them. Pets, young livestock, and wildlife are also at risk. Most fire ants are a characteristic red, but there is a black species. They will eat just about anything, including seeds and other insects. Queens start new colonies by laying tiny white eggs in turf, pasture, or sunny disturbed soil. Queens can live from five to seven years, laying up to 2,000 eggs per day. In spring, adults fly into the air to mate. *Control:* Pour boiling water on top of the mound around 10 A.M., when the queen and workers will be close to the surface. Do not step on the mound!

Flea beetle: These black or brown ¹⁄₁₀-inch-long beetles jump when disturbed. Adults overwinter in soil and emerge in spring when host plants sprout, laying eggs in or on the soil. Larvae are thin white grubs with brown heads that burrow into the soil and eat roots. Adults chew hundreds of tiny holes in leaves, often spreading diseases such as potato scab, blight, and brown rot. There can be as many as four generations a year, but the worst damage is done in spring to young seedlings and transplants. *Control:* Protect seedlings with floating row covers. Spray with neem, rotenone, pyrethrin, sabadilla, or insecticidal soap mixed with pyrethrin. Flea 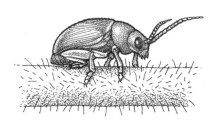 beetles avoid shade, so grow tall plants that shade susceptible plants. Keep your garden free of plant litter—beetles nest there. Plant resistant varieties with hairy or waxy leaves.

Greenhouse whitefly: These tiny mothlike insects are covered with a white, powdery wax. Common on houseplants and in greenhouses everywhere, they appear outdoors in warmer climates. Eggs are laid on the undersides of leaves. Adults and nymphs suck the juices from succu-

lent growth. They feed on fruits, vegetables, and flowers, breeding on tomatoes, potatoes, and squash during the summer and reinfesting greenhouses in fall. *Control:* Spray undersides of leaves with insecticidal soap or superfine horticultural oil, but be careful with seedlings that might react badly. Do a small test first.

Gypsy moth: Females are plump, off-white, about 1 inch long, and unable to fly. The smaller, darker males are strong fliers. The larvae grow to 2½ inches; they are hairy, gray-brown caterpillars with red and blue dots along their bodies. Females

deposit eggs in bark crevices. Larvae appear in the south from May, and from June and July in the north. The larvae feed voraciously, first on tender new leaves, but will ultimately totally defoliate a tree. Pupae are brown, shiny, and teardrop-shaped. Gypsy moths attack more than 500 species of trees and plants, particularly oaks. *Control:* Spray Bt when larvae are young, repeat every 10 to 14 days. Circle tree trunks with sticky bands. Destroy egg masses and pupae by spraying with vegetable oil.

Japanese beetle: These metallic blue-green insects, about ½-inch

long, have bronze wing-covers and a row of white dots at the rear of the abdomen. Adults emerge in early summer, feed on plants, and lay eggs in late August. The larvae are fat white grubs with brown heads; they overwinter deep in the soil and pupate, as the soil warms up, to emerge as adults. The larvae eat roots of grasses and garden plants. Adults attack flowers, fruit, and foliage of just about anything, skeletonizing leaves and often totally defoliating a plant. *Control:* Apply beneficial nematodes to the soil to kill larvae. Milky spore disease provides long-term control. Use Japanese beetle lures and traps to reduce the population.

Leafhopper: There are several species of these ⅒- to ¼-inch-long insects, most notably the potato leafhopper, the beet leafhopper, and the redbanded leafhopper. Mostly green or brown, the redbanded species has gaudy red and blue stripes. All jump fast and fly when disturbed. They cannot survive freezing winters, but migrate north every spring from warmer areas. Eggs are laid in leaves and stems of host plants. Nymphs feed and develop for several weeks, attacking a wide range

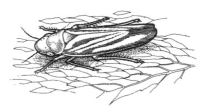

of fruit, vegetable, and flower crops by sucking plant juices, often spreading viral diseases. Depending on species and climate, there can be three to five generations a year. *Control:* Use floating row covers. Spray with insecticidal soap—make sure you wet every insect. Grow resistant varieties.

May and June beetle: These shiny reddish-brown or black insects are about ¾-inch long. Eggs are laid in the soil in spring and hatch in about two weeks. The fat, white, C-shaped larvae feed on the roots and tubers of many plants, including grasses, corn, potatoes, vegetables, and strawberries. Adults eat the leaves of trees and shrubs. Larvae spend from one to three years in the soil, finally pupating to emerge as adults in the spring. They are attracted to light and can be spotted on window screens as well as around porch and deck lights. *Control:* Release beneficial insects and nematodes.

Mealybug: There are long-tailed and short-tailed species of these soft-bodied, ⅒-inch pinkish-white insects. Females of the long-tailed species give birth to live young, while short-tailed females lay more than 500 eggs within a cottonlike mass; after hatching 10 days later, the nymphs crawl off to feed. Male nymphs form a cottony mass and metamorphose into winged adults. Honeydew excretions can cause sooty mold fungus. There can be several generations a year, particularly on indoor or greenhouse plants. Mealybugs suck sap from a wide variety of plants, destroying ornamentals, houseplants, avocados, and fruits. Symptoms include leaves that yellow and drop and premature fruit drop. *Control:* Spray with insecticidal soap or a superfine horticultural oil (not suitable for some plants, so read the label). Release green lacewings. Control ant populations, since ants protect mealybugs from predators. On mature plants, soak cotton swabs with alcohol to remove and kill clusters of insects; spray the plants with water immediately afterward.

Mexican bean beetle: These insects are yellowish-brown to copper in color and about ¼-inch long with 16 small black spots. They are related to the beneficial ladybug group, which have varying numbers of spots, but the bean beetle *always* has 16 spots. Larvae are orange and covered with long,

branched spines. The pale yellowish-orange eggs are always laid in clusters. If you see similar-colored single eggs, they are probably ladybug eggs. Adults overwinter in garden trash and begin laying eggs in May or June, when the temperature reaches 60° F. Eggs hatch in 7 to 14 days. Larvae feed for two to three weeks, then pupate. They may produce as many as three generations a year. *Control:* Protect plants with floating row covers. Plant early-maturing beans to avoid the big late-season beetle population. Handpick and destroy adults and larvae. Spray with insecticidal soap mixed with pyrethrin. Use superfine horticultural oil to kill eggs and larvae. Keep your garden free of plant debris that provides hiding and nesting places.

Mole cricket: There are several species of this insect, ranging from grayish-brown to buff pink. They are large—up to 1¼ inches long— with wide, shovel-like front legs that they use for digging. Eggs are laid in 6-inch-deep underground cells in May. Eggs hatch in June and the nymphs mature by October. They overwinter as adults deep in the soil, then die after they mate and lay eggs. They leave a trail of dead turf grass behind them as they tunnel through the soil, and can uproot young seedlings, often drawing whole plants down into their tunnel. They are excellent fliers, traveling up to 6 miles a night when they're mating. *Control:* Apply the *Steinernema* species of beneficial nematode in spring or fall. St. Augustine grass shows less damage than other types.

Oriental fruit moth: These small, dark, mottled gray moths have a wingspan of about ½ inch. Larvae are pinkish-white ½-inch caterpillars with brown heads. Larvae overwinter in cocoons on tree bark or in soil near trees. Adults emerge in May or June to lay eggs. Larvae hatch in 7 to 10 days and feed on tips of young twigs and ripening fruit at the tops of trees. Larvae also bore into fruit near the stem to feed on the fruit and pit, often leaving no visible entry hole. Adults feed on peach, apricot, nectarine, almond, pear, plum, cherry, and quince trees. *Control:* Hang pheromone traps high in the trees. Spray larvae with Bt. Cultivate the top 3 inches of soil in a wide circle around tree trunks to expose over-wintering larvae.

Peach tree borer: These dark blue, clear-winged, day-flying 1¼-inch moths have a prominent yellow or orange band across the body. Adults emerge from tree trunk burrows from July through late summer or early fall. Eggs are laid on tree trunks or soil near the base of trees. Larvae burrow into tree trunks, leaving a pile of sticky residue of sap, sawdust, and debris by the entrance hole. Borers feed on peach, plum, cherry, nectarine, and other fruit trees. Young trees may lose their vigor or even die if girdled. *Control:* Use  pheromone traps. Inject a liquid solution of beneficial nematodes into the borers' holes. Prevent bark injuries that give borers easy access. Mulch, fertilize, and water trees correctly to avoid weakness.

Pear psylla: Adults are red, brown, or green ⅒-inch-long insects with transparent wings that they fold tentlike over their backs. Overwintering adults emerge in spring from bark crevices and garden debris to lay eggs on fruit buds. Nymphs are almost microscopic, oval, brown or green, and feed on plant juices. Their saliva is toxic to the plants, causing leaves to wilt, yellow, and drop. Nymphs excrete honeydew, which causes black fungus; leaves and fruit blacken. They also transmit a virus that causes pear trees to decline and die. *Control:* Spray lightweight oil in spring just before bud break. Spray insecticidal soap when the first generation hatches. Grow resistant varieties such as red bartlett.

Pickleworm: Adult moths are nocturnal. Their pale wings have broad dark-blue markings around the edges and a wingspan of about 1¼ inches. They also have an odd-looking cluster of hair tufts on the tip of their abdomen. Larvae are greenish-white caterpillars with brown heads; young caterpillars have tiny black spots along their sides. Pickleworms overwinter as pupae in garden debris, emerging as adults in spring to lay yellowish-white eggs singly or in clusters on host plants. They attack all members of the cucurbit family, chewing holes in flowers, leaf buds, and young fruit. Later, larvae tunnel into vine stems and fruit, leaving deposits of green saw-dustlike frass around the entry hole. *Control:* Protect plants with row covers. Spray larvae with Bt, making sure you thoroughly wet all areas of the plants.

Plum curculio: This dark gray-brown beetle has ¼-inch-long lighter markings and a prominent beak. Larvae are white grubs with brown heads. Adults overwinter under rocks, logs, or garden debris and appear when fruit trees bloom and temperatures exceed 65° F. Round white eggs are laid in a crescent-shaped cut in the maturing fruit. Larvae hatch in five days, feed in fruit for two to three weeks, pupate in the soil, and emerge as adults in late summer to early fall. They are capable of pro-ducing two generations a year. Adults eat blossoms, buds, and fruit. Lar-vae burrow into fruit, causing it to drop and rot. Curculio will attack plums, peaches, apples, pears, cherries, quinces, and wild fruits. *Control:* Ground-feeding wild birds eat plum curculio, as will chickens (especially bantams), ducks, and geese. Lay a large cloth under a tree and shake it; curculio will fall off and play dead, and you can make it a reality. Release beneficial nematodes to control next year's curculio population.

Raspberry crown borer: This yellow moth with transparent wings has a black body with four yellow stripes, resembling a yellow jacket. A single egg is laid in the fall on the edges of raspberry and other bramble plant leaves. Larvae fall or climb down to the ground and form an overwintering cell below the surface. During the next growing season larvae chew and bore into the crown of the plant. Larvae pupate inside the fruiting canes in late summer of the second season to mate and lay eggs. Symptoms include loss of vigor, wilting, and browning of canes. *Control:* Destroy wild brambles nearby where borers hide. Handpick eggs from leaves. Apply beneficial nematodes to control grubs in the soil.

Sap beetle: There are several species, most notably the corn sap beetle and the strawberry sap beetle. These ³/₁₆-inch-long black beetles overwinter as adults in woodlots and protected areas, emerging when their target plants near maturity. Larvae damage fruit; they bore into strawberries and cut holes in corn husks to reach the ear. *Control:* Clean up dead and rotting plant material. Plant resistant varieties.

San Jose scale: Females have a gray shell about ¹/₁₀-inch long with a yellow nipplelike projection in the center. The male is smaller, darker, and pear-shaped. They become full-grown around the time that fruit trees bloom. Females give birth to live young. The active nymphs crawl around for several hours, then settle on bark, leaves, or fruit to feed. There can be up to six generations per year. They attack most deciduous fruit and nut trees, shade trees, and ornamental shrubs. *Control:* Examine prunings carefully to spot live insects. Spray trees with superfine horticultural or dormant oil before bud break in spring, thoroughly coating all branches.

Spider mite: They are indeed spiders, but only the size of a grain of salt. The two-spotted spider mite (your magnifying glass comes in handy) has two dark spots on its back, while the overwintering adult is orange. They overwinter in garden trash and move onto plants in early spring to lay eggs, which hatch in two to three days. Nymphs grow to adulthood in 7 to 10 days. They attack houseplants, ornamentals, grapes, almonds, strawberries, peppers, and cucurbits (cucumbers, squash, melons, and gourds). Mites suck juices from the undersides of leaves, causing the leaves to yellow and drop. Palm leaves  turn dusty gray. Mites weave a small, fine web. *Control:* Release green lacewing beneficials. Spray mites with insecticidal soap. Spray fruit trees at bud break with superfine horticultural oil. On mature plants, dislodge mites with a strong spray of water. Mulch and mist indoor plants regularly; mites dislike humidity. A sprayable mixture of flour and water will dry and stick mites to leaves. When mites are dead, wash plants to remove flour residue.

Spittle bug: There are several species of these ¼- to ½-inch black or brown bugs with froglike faces; they are sometimes called froghoppers. Overwinter eggs hatch from April to June. Larvae are yellow, pink, or green and wingless. Upon hatching, they surround themselves with a mass of white froth. Both adults and nymphs suck sap from a very wide range of plants, favoring strawberries, legumes, and meadow forage crops; one species attacks chrysanthemums. *Control:* Release beneficial insects. Clean up the garden in fall, removing debris, especially weedy grasses.

Squash bug: Adults are brown to black bugs with orange or brown markings around the abdomen. They emit an unpleasant odor when crushed. Adults hibernate in garden trash or other shelter and emerge in spring to lay eggs on the undersides of leaves. Shiny brown eggs are laid singly or in groups. Nymphs feed in clusters all summer, molting several

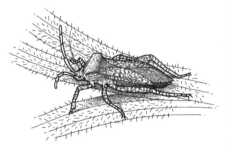

times. Adults and nymphs feed on all members of the cucurbit family—gourds, pumpkins, cucumbers, melons, squash (especially winter squash)—by sucking plant juices. Leaves, stems, even whole plants turn black and die. Plants that survive an attack will not bear fruit. *Control:* Protect plants with floating row covers. Spray 5 percent rotenone. Dust serious infestations with sabadilla. Place a board flat on the ground near the plants; bugs shelter underneath. Lift the board first thing in the morning and destroy the bugs. Rotate your plantings next year.

Squash vine borer: These metallic brown moths are 1 to 1½ inches long with bright red abdomens ringed with black stripes. Adults emerge in spring and lay single eggs along the stems near the base of cucurbits—squash, gourds, pumpkins, cucumbers, and melons. The eggs are brown, flat ovals. Upon hatching, the larvae bore into the vines, causing wilting or death of the plant. Look for a gooey sawdustlike substance oozing from holes in stems near the ground. Larvae feed for six to eight weeks, then pupate in the soil to overwinter. *Control:* Protect plants with floating row covers. Dust with rotenone and repeat weekly. Inject beneficial nematodes into the stem to kill larvae. Early or late plantings avoid infestations. In fall, clean up and burn vine residue. Lightly till garden to bring cocoons to the surface.

Stinkbug: There are several species, including the harlequin bug. (These are examples of true bugs.) They are about ½-inch long and shield-shaped, with triangles on their backs. Most are brown or green; harlequin bugs are red and black. Adults overwinter under garden debris and wood, emerging in spring to lay 300 to 500 eggs at bloom time on the undersides of leaves. Eggs hatch in five to seven  days. Nymphs develop to adulthood in four to six weeks. Two generations a year are possible. Stinkbugs attack leaves, blossoms, fruit, and seeds of brassica (cabbage family) plants, other vegetables, small fruits, and trees. Symptoms include light-colored hard spots on tomatoes or seedless bean pods; peaches will be "catfaced" (scarred and dimpled), and pears will have deep depressions. White or yellow blotches are left on brassica plants. *Control:* Destroy eggs by hand; they are distinctive, small white pegs attached to black loops, standing on end and lined in double rows. In season, insecticidal soap may be effective.

Tent caterpillar: Adults are yellowish-brown moths with a wingspan of about 1 to 1½ inches and two light stripes on the wings. Larvae are hairy, gray-brown caterpillars with black dots and lighter markings. Overwinter eggs hatch in early spring about the time that apple and cherry leaves unfold. Larvae collect in the fork of a tree and spin a dense, weblike tent in which they hide during the day; they leave the tent at night to feed on leaves. They attack a wide range of fruit and other deciduous trees. Larvae pupate in white cocoons on tree trunks or in garden debris. *Control:* Spray Bt *kurstaki* when larvae are young. Wind webs, caterpillars and all, onto a broomstick; then rub them off into a bucket of soapy water. Prune and burn infested branches.

Thrips: Get out the magnifying glass. Thrips are several species of tiny torpedo-shaped insects that are yellow, brown, or black and only ⅟₅₀- to ⅟₂₅-inch long. They do extensive damage to roses, and are particularly attracted to white blossoms; they can be found in the center of the blossom, feeding on pollen. When disturbed, they quickly jump or fly away on narrow wings. They appear quickly in hot, dry weather to lay eggs on plants. Various species attack onions and a wide range of flowers, fruits, and trees. Symptoms include leaves with a silvery sheen. *Control:* Spray with insecticidal soap. Remove garden trash at the end of the season to kill overwintering thrips.

Tomato hornworm: This large moth has mottled brown and gray wings and five orange spots on its body. The wingspan is up to 5 inches. Smooth, round, pale green eggs are laid singly on leaves of tomatoes, potatoes, peppers, and eggplant. The larva is a green caterpillar up to 4

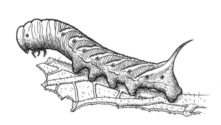

inches long; it has eight white V markings along its back and a black horn on its tail. Adults emerge in June or July to lay eggs. The larvae feed for about a month, then pupate in the soil. Larvae will occasionally feed on other plants, including alfalfa, grape, okra, pea, and squash. *Control:* Spray with Bt when larvae are small and repeat weekly. Till the soil after harvest to destroy pupae.

Wireworm: The adults are slender, dark brown or black beetles about ½-inch long, often called click beetles: if you flip them on their backs, they click as they right themselves. Larvae are wiry, about 1 to 1½ inches long, orange or yellow with narrow lighter bands marking the segments. Adults overwinter deep in the soil, emerging in spring to lay eggs at the base of plants. The larvae can spend five or six years feeding on roots and tubers in the soil. They are very destructive pests of potatoes and carrots. Adults feed on nectar and pollen, and males like to perch on grass stalks. *Control:* Control weeds. Use nongrain cover crops, such as soybeans or vetches; turn under in late fall or early winter. Apply parasitic nematodes to the soil.

INSECT CONTROL

Throughout this book, prevention is emphasized as the best way to avoid infestations of harmful insects. Healthy soil, repellent plants mixed with insect favorites, and diversified gardens are undoubtedly effective. Even so, every gardener inevitably experiences that sinking feeling when a horde of insects descends (or ascends from the soil below) and starts chomping on a flower or vegetable. At this point, action becomes necessary.

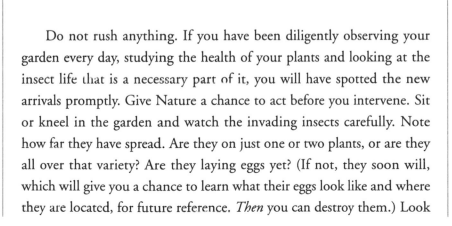

Do not rush anything. If you have been diligently observing your garden every day, studying the health of your plants and looking at the insect life that is a necessary part of it, you will have spotted the new arrivals promptly. Give Nature a chance to act before you intervene. Sit or kneel in the garden and watch the invading insects carefully. Note how far they have spread. Are they on just one or two plants, or are they all over that variety? Are they laying eggs yet? (If not, they soon will, which will give you a chance to learn what their eggs look like and where they are located, for future reference. *Then* you can destroy them.) Look with special care for any predator activity. Predators may not arrive immediately, and unless the attack is doing disastrous damage you can probably afford to wait for a day.

Positively identify the pest involved. Make absolutely sure that what you're worried about is really a *pest,* not one of the many beneficial look-alikes. Consider its life cycle: how quickly does it reproduce, where does it lay its eggs, what are its predators? Then, and *only* then, should you

KEEPING A GARDEN NOTEBOOK

When you are busy with the daily activities of your garden it's hard to think about record-keeping. But no matter how hard you try to remember all the details of your garden, time can (and will!) blur them into a confusing jumble. It is easy to forget exactly where you planted what, which variety of seed you used, what insects appeared when, what controls you used, when, and how successful they were.

In addition to all that information, there are details of companion planting, succession planting, soil amendments (how much, how often, and where?), and new approaches to insect control. You need to keep track of all these things because if you don't, you may forget some successful method or repeat the same mistakes next year or the year after that.

The only way to be sure is to keep a garden planning and record book. You will find the notes and information useful, even fascinating, a few years down the road. Sketch your layouts to help with rotation planting. Jot down what mulches or amendments you applied, where, how much, and when. Keep track of all the insects, beneficial, neutral, and harmful, noting when they appeared and vanished. List the plants or varieties that succeeded, and those that didn't.

Try to get into the habit of noting daily weather conditions such as minimum and maximum temperatures, how much rainfall (and how long you ran your irrigation system), and anything else that could affect plant and insect life cycles. Your garden notebook should be permanent and easily handled. You can use a page-a-day diary or a preindexed book, but avoid looseleaf binders because pages tend to get torn out and lost. Make sure you can live with your garden notebook, and it will help you create the best possible garden.

plan your attack strategy. Decide whether you should use a botanical spray or dust, diatomaceous earth, a dormant oil, a physical trap, some form of biological control, or beneficial insects. Bear in mind that some of these measures can, if used carelessly, kill beneficial insects as well as the target pest.

ORGANIC SPRAYS AND DUSTS

In a good garden-management program, using substances that will kill insects is the absolute last line of defense. Don't do it until you are certain a real problem exists that cannot be dealt with in any other way. Then do everything possible to ensure that the risk to beneficial insects is minimized.

Protect yourself, too. Just because a spray or dust is "organic" does not mean that it cannot harm humans. Please read, and follow, the instructions that come with whatever you use. Wear gloves, a long-sleeved shirt or jacket, and face and eye protection if they're called for. Keep children and pets well away from the area while you're spraying or dusting and for a safe time afterward.

Even though a control is organic, it can still be harmful to humans and animals.

SOAPS AND BOTANICAL CONTROLS: Botanical controls are derived from the roots, leaves, or flowers of plants that have insecticidal properties. They are short-lived in the environment; sunlight breaks them down into harmless by-products. However, the toxic effect of botanical controls can last from three hours to several weeks, depending on the substance used. They can be extremely effective when used properly, so be sure to apply the correct spray or dust for your specific need.

Start with the mildest and safest of the substances that are recommended against your target insect. If that substance proves ineffective after you have given it time to work, only then should you escalate your attack to more potent materials. Buy a good-quality spray bottle for liquid sprays. Mark it permanently with the name of the substance and keep it for that substance *exclusively*. Dispose of leftover mixes where they will do no harm; treat them as toxic materials and deal with them accordingly.

Safe and effective insecticidal soaps are among the best natural insect controls. They are made from fatty acids derived from animals and plants. Soaps control soft-bodied insects that come in contact with the wet spray. Crops can be sprayed right up until harvest time, and the residues break down quickly with no long-term effect on the environment.

ROTENONE is a root extract of the derris plant family, which grows in the tropics. It is a broad-spectrum insecticide, an insect stomach poison. This means that the insect must ingest it before it takes effect. It will kill most beneficial insects too, so be careful with rotenone. It is toxic to fish and can kill birds. It is moderately toxic to humans and swine. Do not spray it near any body of water. It is deadly to aphids, cabbageworms, Mexican bean beetles, apple maggots, Colorado potato beetle, cherry fruit fly, carrot rust fly, leafhoppers, red spider mites, leaf rollers, and others.

SABADILLA is both a contact and stomach poison, which means that it kills insects you spray it on *and* those that eat sprayed plant materials. Therefore, it's effective against a wide range of insects. It is made from the seeds of a lilylike South American plant. It is toxic to honeybees and some mammals, and it causes susceptible people to suffer a violent allergic reaction.

PYRETHRIN is derived from pyrethrum daisies, a member of the chrysanthemum family. Its effects are short-lived—it is rendered inactive by sunlight within 24 hours after application. For this reason, it's best applied late in the day, preferably after sunset, so that it can have as long as possible to work. It is a contact and stomach poison used to control aphids, cabbage loopers, codling moths, Colorado potato beetles, Mexican bean beetles, spider mites, whiteflies, leafhoppers, and others. Do not confuse pyrethrin with synthetic pyrethroids, which have a long residual life and are highly toxic to beneficial insects.

NEEM is a relatively new botanical control. Its active ingredient, azadirachtin, is extracted from the seeds of the neem tree, which is found in south Asia, Africa, Australia, and India. Neem interrupts the insect's growth cycle, causing death to larval and pupal stages. It is effective against Colorado potato beetles, Mexican bean beetles, corn earworms, cucumber beetles, and flea beetles. Once they have ingested it, insects stop feeding and will die within a few days. So don't expect insects to keel over immediately: watch them, and you will see them stop eating while they continue to live for a few days. Neem also acts as a repellent, driving insects from the sprayed area. It is not harmful to most beneficial insects and lasts for 3 to 10 days. It works against many common insect pests. Time your applications for early to midmorning or late afternoon. Neem is only mildly toxic to humans and beneficial insects.

DIATOMACEOUS EARTH

Available as a dust or wettable powder, diatomaceous earth is the ground-up remains of one-celled freshwater algae called diatoms. It kills insects by piercing the skin of those traveling through it, or by puncturing the internal organs of those insects that consume it. It is more effective under dry conditions. Because its killing action is mechanical rather than poisonous, insects have not developed immunity to it.

Use diatomaceous earth as a barrier to crawling pests such as slugs, snails, and earwigs. Dusted on damp foliage it controls soft-bodied insects including thrips and aphids. Avoid breathing the dust: always wear a dust mask when applying it. Apply it early in the morning.

RYANIA, made from the resin of the plant *Ryania speciosa,* is a stomach poison that kills insects that eat leaves. It is also effective against corn earworms, borers, and codling moths. Gentle to beneficial insects, it will not injure plant tissue, but it is toxic to mammals (including humans) and marine life.

QUASSIA is a selective and safe botanical from the South American bitterwood (quassia) tree. It is effective against most soft-bodied insects, but it also harms beneficial ones. Quassia bark chips are available in some health food stores as a medicinal herb, and some people believe that the bark chips are more effective on the ground around plants than sprayed directly on them.

DORMANT OIL NEVER SLEEPS: A 3 percent dormant oil spray is, like diatomaceous earth, a mechanical (rather than poisonous) pest control method. It encases a whole tree in an envelope of oil that suffocates insects. Sprayed when dormant during the late winter or early spring, a tree can still get enough oxygen from its roots (instead of through its leaves) and will not be harmed.

Dormant oils are effective against a host of sucking and chewing insects, including aphids, thrips, whiteflies, pear psylla, red spider mites, and various forms of scale. It also kills the eggs of oriental fruit moth, and various forms of leaf roller and cankerworm. If there is a lot of moss or lichen on the tree, under which insects may hide, scrape it off before spraying. Do not apply the regular kind of dormant oil when buds are opening or it may cause leaf burn, leaf drop, and fruit drop.

Dormant oil should not be sprayed when buds are opening as it may damage fruit development.

Focus on the trunk, large branches, and crotches where insects hide their eggs. You must cover the whole tree, as insect eggs are often laid on the tips of branches. Don't spray on a windy day, or you will get drenched. It can be used on all trees, shrubs, and evergreens, but not on blue spruce because it causes discoloration.

A newer type of dormant oil, ultrafine horticultural spray oils, can be used in late winter or early spring, or as a summer spray on fruit trees. This type of oil is also effective on roses, annual and perennial flowers, blueberries, strawberries, and grapes. Unlike the other dormant oils, ultrafine spray oils can be used on plants several times during the summer. They repel insects such as leaf miners and greenhouse whiteflies. Beneficial or harmful insects that land on a tree or plant *after* spraying are not affected.

BIOLOGICAL CONTROLS

Biological controls, the least toxic pest-fighting method, are often effective against only one insect or class of insects. Because they are host-specific, they don't harm beneficial insects or the environment. The limitation to their use is that they must be applied when the target insects are in the early larval stage (for example, young caterpillars) or they will not be effective. Fully developed larvae need to eat the pesticide for it to work, and at this stage of their life they eat less as they prepare to turn into pupae. Anyone who has a garden, stable, or chicken house can benefit from biological pest control.

Microbial controls are insect pathogens or diseases. These pathogens fight bugs by damaging their ability to reproduce or develop, or simply by killing them. Many of these pathogens are already present in healthy gardens, but by encouraging a disease that's already there or introducing a new one, you can do battle with specific pests.

Bacteria are a very efficient way to spread diseases among pest insects. One form of bacteria, *Bacillus thuringiensis* (commonly known as Bt), has become a favorite of organic growers and farmers. Bt (pronounced bee-tee) controls a wide range of leaf-eating caterpillars, including gypsy moths, tent caterpillars, cabbageworms, tomato hornworms, diamondback moth larvae, green looper worms, and sod

THE *FRIENDLY* NEMATODE

Parasitic nematodes are totally safe biological controls. They should not be confused with *harmful* nematodes, such as the golden root-knot nematode, that attack plants. Parasitic nematodes are host-specific, targeting only soil-dwelling insect pests. They are effective against a large range of insects, including armyworms, cutworms, peach tree borers, mole crickets, sod webworms, Japanese beetle larvae, carrot weevils, onion maggots, and sweet potato weevils. Nematodes are killed by ultraviolet light and need moisture, so apply them in the evening to well-watered ground that is free of mulch or thatch. The soil temperature should be 60 to 65° F. If you have a serious infestation of harmful insects in your soil, you may need to make more than one application.

webworms. Bt cannot harm insects that don't eat it, so it kills only what you want it to. For example, spraying your cabbage will not hurt monarch butterflies, because their larvae do not feed on cabbage.

Several varieties of Bt are available to fight specific pests. Bt *san diego* is highly effective against Colorado potato beetle. Beetle larvae chewing on sprayed leaves stop eating immediately and die within a few days. Bt *israelensis* kills the larvae of fungus gnats, blackflies, and mosquitoes. Bt *kurstaki* is said to be 10 times more effective than regular Bt.

Time your spraying of Bt with care. It loses its effectiveness after a few days—it deteriorates in sunlight—so you may need to apply it more than once to kill the caterpillars you missed the first time around. And do not spray it indiscriminately all over the garden because it will kill the larvae of harmless and beneficial insects as well. Spray it only on the plant or plants that have a problem.

Milky spore disease is another naturally occurring bacterium. It kills the grubs of Japanese beetles, rose chafer, and some May and June beetles, which burrow in grassy areas. By applying milky spore powder in spring or fall to a mown area, in small patches a few feet apart, these damaging insects are killed. It is harmless to humans and pets. It is often applied with parasitic nematodes, which also kill the target pests. One application is said to last for at least 20 years.

HOMEMADE CONTROLS

Long before chemical or biological ways were found to fight harmful insects, gardeners made their own teas and infusions. Many homemade sprays and dusts are extremely effective, and they're easy to make. Hot-tasting or strong-smelling ingredients are very powerful bug controls, and by adding a horticultural spreader-sticker to foliar sprays, you will increase their effectiveness. Some of these products, such as Nu-Film-17 or fish oil spreader-sticker, have further beneficial effects of their own, including growth stimulation and stress reduction. They can also be used as soil conditioners.

Sprays are made by liquefying ingredients in a blender, straining the mash through a double layer of cheesecloth, and diluting the liquid in a pressure sprayer or spray bottle. When blending herbs, add a couple of cups of water and a few drops of spreader-sticker. If you're hesitant to make some of these concoctions in your kitchen blender, buy a cheap blender just for this purpose, or pick up a used blender at a yard sale.

Most homemade sprays are made from plants you can grow yourself. Parsnip roots contain a substance that kills fruit flies, Mexican bean beetles, pea aphids, and mosquito larvae. Garlic sprays are popular on the agricultural market, but you can make your own to deal with all sorts of insects. Blend two whole garlic bulbs, mashed, with 4 teaspoons of hot peppers and a few drops of spreader-sticker. Strain and mix with a gallon of hot water. This spray is very effective against tree caterpillars.

For a good all-purpose insect spray, blend three hot peppers, one large onion, one whole bulb of garlic, and five pinches of pipe tobacco with just enough water to cover. Liquefy this mixture and place it in a covered container overnight. The next day, strain the mash, add a couple of drops of spreader-sticker, and dilute with an equal amount of water. For heavy infestations, spray this solution three times a day for two days. Repeat an application if it is washed off by heavy rain. As a protectant, you can bury the remaining mash under your roses and fruit trees.

For roses bothered by aphids, mix shallots or green onions in a blender with an equal amount of water. Strain and spray on the affected plants. Hot peppers are wonderful bug destroyers. Take one garlic clove, two or three red-hot peppers, half a mild green bell pepper, and half an onion. Blend with water and spreader-sticker, let the mixture stand for a day, then strain and spray. Ground-up pods of cayenne peppers mixed with a wetting agent (a couple of drops of dish detergent) and water, then strained and sprayed, will discourage and even kill pests. This mixture works on ants, spiders, cabbageworms, caterpillars, and tomato hornworms.

Greenflies and caterpillars are discouraged by a tea made from tomato leaves or stinging nettles. Chop the leaves coarsely and infuse them in hot water. Let the mixture stand until it's cool, strain, and spray. Cedar tea, made from cedar chips or sawdust, will deter Mexican bean beetles, Colorado potato beetles, red spider mites, mealybugs, cucumber beetles, and squash bugs.

By using herbal mixtures against specific bugs, you can create very effective controls with natural ingredients. For aphids, try a mixture of pennyroyal, spearmint, southernwood, tansy, and garlic. Tree borers run when you spray them with a mixture of garlic, tansy, and anise. Against carrot flies, try a mixture of rosemary, sage, garlic, and coriander. Cabbage moths flee from a combination of mint, hyssop, rosemary, thyme, sage, and catnip. Against cabbage maggots, use rosemary, sage, and wormwood. Colorado potato beetles shrink when sprayed with horseradish, nettle, and flax.

Tansy plants are effective deterrents, and the leaves work well as a spray. Blend, strain, and spray on cucumber beetles (both spotted and striped) and cutworms. Marigold leaf spray is good against eelworms; mixed with rosemary and summer savory it is effective against Mexican bean beetles. For harmful nematodes, try a mixture of marigolds and yarrow. To beat whiteflies, spray a combination of marigold and nasturtium.

Flea beetles dislike a spray made from wormwood, mint, and catnip. Fruit tree moths hate a spray of southernwood, and plum curculios can't stand a garlic spray. If snails are a problem, spray a concoction of rosemary, sage, and wormwood. Squash bugs respond well to a garlic, tansy, and nasturtium spray. To keep tomatoes free of tomato hornworms, try a mixture of borage, marigolds, and basil. Wireworms will scurry when sprayed with a garlic, thyme, tansy, and pennyroyal mixture. For mites, make a spray with 1 tablespoon of buttermilk, ½ cup of flour, and 2½ quarts of water.

Cabbageworms are deterred by a dusting of powdered sugar, and bugs are immobilized by a sprinkle of flour. Scale insects on fruit trees can be smothered with ground mustard seed mixed with a superfine horticultural oil; spray in the fall. Slugs are killed by a shake of salt, and a cup of strong coffee sprinkled on plants repels red spider mites. Colorado potato bugs are deterred by horseradish mixed with water, and ground asparagus works well as a nematode repellent. Lime sprinkled in infested areas discourages sow bugs.

TRAPS AND BARRIERS

Traps are a useful and nonpoisonous way to control and monitor insects. Some are simply sticky surfaces, often in a color that attracts target species. They work like old-fashioned flypaper with a modern twist—our knowledge of what colors attract insects. Other more sophisticated traps use pheromones, or scents that female insects use to attract mating males. Homemade traps use food baits.

Barriers of gossamer-light, spun-bonded fabrics, called row covers (see below), prevent insects from seeing or reaching susceptible plants and are particularly effective during the early part of the growing season. Young plants can be protected until they're strong enough to resist insect attack.

FLOATING ROW COVERS: It is better to keep insects off your plants than deal with them later. There is no easier way to do this than to use floating row covers, and it's hard to understand why more gardeners don't use them. These light fabrics are available in a range of lengths and widths, from 5 feet wide and 25 feet long to rolls 50 feet wide and 500 feet long. There are three weights. One is so gossamer-light that it can be rested loosely on top of young seedlings; the plants lift it as they grow. The heavier materials need to be supported by wire hoops pushed into the ground to form a tunnel. They offer moderate frost protection as well.

Row covers permit light and moisture to enter, but exclude flying insects. Ideally, a drip irrigation line is laid near the plants. The edges of the covers are secured to the ground with U-shaped wire ground staples or piles of earth. There are several brands; the best known are Reemay

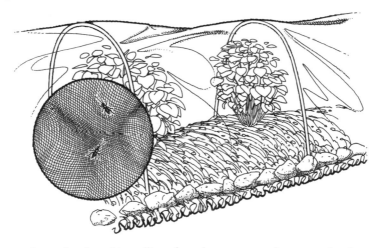

Pests can't attack vulnerable seedlings through a row cover, but sun and moisture penetrate easily.

and Agribon. The most durable is Tufbell, which is reinforced with nylon threads and will last for many years. The lightest fabrics tend to degrade in sunlight or get torn after one or two seasons.

If you place a row cover over insect-susceptible crops, such as squash or potatoes, you leave it on until the plants flower. You should then remove it for a few days to permit pollination to take place. Squash bugs, cucumber beetles, and Colorado potato beetles are usually past their peak by then. If not, you can replace the cover once you are reasonably sure no injurious insects are on the plants. If you are not sure, put a few praying mantises under the cover, too. They will rapidly search out any lurking bugs.

In early spring, and later in the year when frosts are a possibility, the heavier fabrics offer protection down to 24° F. By trapping heat—they can raise soil temperatures by as much as 10° F—they provide a suitably warm environment for heat-lovers such as peppers and eggplant. For some crops, row covers can make *any* other form of insect control unnecessary.

PHYSICAL TRAPS: Well known for their effectiveness, liquid traps catch large numbers of destructive snails and slugs. Fill a saucer or other shallow container with stale beer or sugar water and place it on the ground under your plants. Some gardeners add a little flour. Snails and slugs cannot resist; they crawl in and drown. Ants are drawn to sugar water, too. Add the bodies to your compost heap and let Nature take its course.

A cabbage leaf, concave side downward, can be laid on the ground in the evening. Overnight all sorts of bugs, including cutworms, slugs, and other night-feeders, will huddle underneath. Gather them up and destroy them in the morning. Wooden boards of any size or shape, left lying on the ground, will reap a similar harvest. Earwigs and various beetles find the undersides of boards attractive hiding places. But don't forget to clear your trap in the morning, or the trap will turn into a bug breeding center.

Japanese beetles are drawn to geranium oil and the color yellow. Coat a piece of yellow board or cardboard with Tangle-Trap or Stick-Em (sticky coatings made for this purpose) and sprinkle a little geranium oil on it. Scrape the trapped bugs off it periodically and destroy them.

Other baits include citronella oil, which draws fruit flies, and molasses, citrus fruit, salt, or soap, which grasshoppers love.

Tree pests have a fatal attraction for anything sweet. Codling moths can be caught by the score in a small bucket containing molasses, sugar, and water. Hang it in the tree and remove the drowned insects frequently. Codling moths also go for sassafras oil mixed with sawdust, or molasses mixed with yeast. Apple maggot flies can be trapped on a red sphere (like a giant apple) coated with Tangle-Trap or Stick-Em and hung in the tree. Red plastic or wood spheres can be purchased from organic suppliers, or you can make your own.

Commercial light traps, commonly known as zappers, are very effective against a variety of night-flying moths and beetles. They kill indiscriminately, however, and will eliminate beneficial insects as well as harmful bugs. Like sticky traps, they can be a useful way to monitor insect populations. A trap will often catch a harmful bug before you notice its presence in the garden.

PHEROMONE TRAPS: Insects are preoccupied with food and sex. Insect pheromones that mimic the scents females use to attract mates can be synthesized. Unlike sticky traps, pheromones are species-specific: they attract only the bug you want to catch, and beneficials are unaffected. Pheromone traps are available for several species, including codling moths, oriental fruit moth, and peach tree borer.

Some gardeners claim that pheromone traps can attract insects to an area that they might otherwise miss.

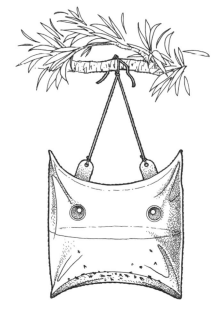

Few insects can resist the scent of pheromones that mimic those of the female.

This fear does not seem to be well substantiated, however, and while harmful insects may miss an individual tree, their ability to home in on target plants and trees is well known to most growers. Because pheromone traps are species-specific and many harmful insects are night-feeders and therefore hard to spot, it's probably better to use their protection for susceptible plantings.

WILDLIFE *in* the GARDEN

Insects and spiders are only part of a garden's animal kingdom. Many wild creatures have adapted their ways to human civilization, having learned that a garden is a rich source of food. On the harmful side, rabbits and deer come immediately to mind, but many more critters quietly visit the garden without leaving a trace. Because the majority eat harmful insects, organic gardeners welcome their presence.

People who are new to gardening or country life are sometimes startled or alarmed by these visitors. But just as most insects can safely be regarded as your friends, so too can many forms of wildlife. By learning more about what these creatures do for us, you will soon see that they are an essential part of the balanced ecosystem you should strive to create in your garden.

In fact, it's in our interest to go beyond passive acceptance of their presence. If we plan ways to attract birds, frogs, salamanders, even snakes and bats, our gardens will be enriched. After all, these creatures wish us no harm. On the contrary, most of them would prefer never to see us at all. Their whole lives are spent relentlessly pursuing four imperatives: evade predators, find safe sources of food, breed, and raise young.

Even wildlife that we consider harmful should be regarded with kindness. Deer that chew a prized rosebush to the ground or munch their way down a row of young lettuce are not doing this with any malicious intent: they simply need to eat. Rabbits that decimate a bed of cabbage are not thrill-seeking vandals: they are just trying to survive. It is hard not to be angry when this sort of damage occurs, but the blame belongs more to us for failing to keep them away. We have resources at our disposal that can be used to outwit the most wily intruder. It is up to us to use our intelligence and live in harmony with the creatures around us.

BIRDS

Our feathered friends are among the most capable pest controllers. They know where to look to find insect food, and their need is constant. A nesting pair of birds with a brood of young to feed run themselves ragged trying to keep up with the insistent cries of their young. It's said that some adult birds can lose as much as a quarter of their body weight during nesting season.

While birds will naturally gravitate toward the multiple food sources of a fertile garden, there are several things you can do to encourage more of them to visit with frequency. Birds need food, shelter from predators, and places to nest. Hedges, shrubs, and trees of carefully chosen varieties will provide all three. Many types of berries are particularly valuable food in cold weather, when other foods are not available. Dense hedges and many trees provide nighttime roosts, shelter, and nest sites.

Water is a constant attraction. If you can provide fresh water throughout the year, particularly when other water sources are frozen solid, you will be blessed with birds. Poultry keepers use a special electrically heated device, a flat-topped galvanized metal disk, that keeps water just above freezing. If you can manage the hookup, you could have one of these in your garden with a large, shallow dish of water on it.

Nest boxes come in a variety of sizes and shapes and can be placed all around your yard. Birds have specific preferences for height and location, and you can—to some extent—control your potential tenants by the location of the box, the size of the entry hole, and whether or not it has a perch by the hole. The bird list that follows provides details.

It is true that some birds like fruit as much as you do. Dwarf trees and rows of fruit bushes can be protected with plastic bird-netting. For individual clusters, you can use paper or transparent plastic bags held in place with wooden clothespins and open at the bottom to allow drainage and prevent condensation. Sticky materials such as Tree Tangle-foot discourage birds from perching where you don't want them. Under *no* circumstances should it ever be necessary to even *consider* killing birds.

BIRDS YOU CAN ATTRACT: Bluebirds will prey on grasshoppers, moths, crickets, beetles, ants, caterpillars, worms, spiders, millipedes, and centipedes. They nest in tree holes, particularly in apple orchards, but they will make use of appropriate nest boxes. Eastern bluebirds like a floor dimension of 4 inches by 4 inches, while mountain and western bluebirds prefer 5 inches by 5 inches. From the top of the floor to the bottom of the hole should be about 6 inches. The hole for eastern bluebirds should be 1½ inches; for mountain and western blue-birds, 1⁹⁄₁₆ inches. Do not affix a perch as this encourages spar-

BIRD FEEDERS

Feeders are a well-known and successful way to bring birds from near and far. Bear in mind, however, that a feeder is something of a commitment. If birds get used to a steady supply of food they can come to depend on it. If you suddenly cut off that supply when you go away, or if you just lose interest, several species will be hard-pressed to find a replacement. In the depths of winter, this can be life-threatening for them.

A feeder can be no more than a flat board on a post—preferably with an edge around it to prevent seed from blowing off, and a drain hole in one corner. Hanging feeders are a little harder for squirrels to raid, and there seems to be an endless list of devices to keep them away (some of which work, at least for a while). Winter feed can include a variety of seeds, suet, corn ears, or peanut butter mixed with flour and cornmeal; this can be spread on wire hardware cloth, or placed in a can hung from a branch.

rows, and bluebirds do not need a perch. Provide drainage holes in the bottom of the box, and small ventilation holes at the top of the sides or back. The roof should have a 2-inch overhang. Mount the box on a pole or tree, at least 4 feet from the ground. Ready-made nest boxes are available from the North American Bluebird Society, among others.

Bluejays are loud and pretty aggressive and may rob the nests of other birds. About three-quarters of their diet is vegetable matter such as seeds, acorns, and nuts; they also eat insects, spiders, snails, mice, amphibians, and even fish. The **brown thrasher** feeds mainly on insects, including beetles, caterpillars, weevils, worms, grasshoppers, leafhoppers, and wasps. They are unlikely to use a nest box, but will be drawn to dense thickets of hedge or vine.

Cardinals are shy birds that will nest just about anywhere. Their diet is quite varied and includes aphids, ants, beetles, caterpillars, cicadas, grasshoppers, leafhoppers, moths, and worms. **Catbirds** eat ants, beetles, and caterpillars in the spring, switching to fruits and vegetables in the summer and fall. **Chickadees** feed on insects and insect eggs, including ants, aphids, bark

Female cardinals have a dark brown color. Both sexes are accomplished singers.

beetles, flies, scales, spiders, wasps, and weevils. A nest box for chickadees with a 1-inch entry hole will keep out larger birds.

The great crested **flycatcher** is found in the eastern half of the United States. It feeds almost exclusively on insects, including caterpillars, grasshoppers, May beetles, sawflies, stinkbugs, and weevils. They may be tempted by a nest box with a 2-inch entry hole placed about 25 feet above the ground. The slate-colored **junco,** actually a race of the dark-eyed junco species, is related to the sparrows. They prefer to nest in woodland and pasture areas and are completely beneficial, eating click beetles, grasshoppers, leafhoppers, and ants during the summer.

The **mockingbird** is an effective insect destroyer, although it will sometimes attack fruit trees and berry bushes. Its diet includes ants, caterpillars, flies, grasshoppers, spiders, wasps, and weevils. You may need to protect your own fruit, but you can attract this friendly bird with wild grape and Juneberry. **Orioles** are found all over the United States. Of the nine species, the Baltimore oriole, orchard oriole, and Bullock's oriole (found mainly in the west) are the best known. Their diet is mainly insects, including gypsy moths, cankerworms, and brown-tail moths, but they will attack grapes.

Owls, with their unusual front-facing eyes and silent flight, are superb hunters. They eat insects, rats, mice, and other small mammals, lizards, and worms. Shy and nocturnal, some species can be persuaded to use a nest box. They are big birds with rambunctious chicks, so they need a large container such as a plastic (not metal) 55-gallon drum or a large wooden box with a 6-inch entrance hole, a wooden sunshade to keep the inside cool, and an entrance perch. It should be mounted high in a tree and firmly secured. Barn owls are smaller and may use an 8-inch-square wooden box with a 3¼ inch opening. Line the floor of owl nest boxes with shredded wood bark.

The **phoebe** species (three in the United States) are members of the flycatcher family. Phoebes eat ants, beetles, caterpillars, grasshoppers, moths, ticks, and weevils. They can be lured to your garden with a nest box.

Purple martins feed constantly on beetles, dragonflies, flies, mosquitoes, squash bugs, weevils, and some wasps and bees. Migrating from their winter habitat near the equator, purple martins arrive in the north by spring. To attract them, you must provide a properly designed and constructed house in the right location.

Native Americans lured purple martins to villages by providing hollowed-out gourds as nests.

Each nesting pair needs a compartment 6 inches by 6 inches, with a 2½-inch circular opening 1 inch above the floor. How many compartments you provide is up to you. If you are at all handy, you can make one yourself; if not, you can buy a ready-made martin house. In either case, make sure it is painted white. This attracts the birds and keeps them cool in warm weather. You can place grass, leaves, and bits of twigs inside to make them feel at home. Finally, remember that martins capture insects on the wing, so place their house out in the open so they can glide back to it.

Among the 18 varieties of **sparrow** found in the United States, the house sparrow, American tree sparrow, and chipping sparrow are among the most common. Members of the finch family, they eat insects, seeds, and berries. They are not above plucking young seedlings, either. These aggressive little birds can drive away bluebirds and purple martins, so they are a mixed blessing in the garden.

Swallows are welcomed as harbingers of spring, and they are good to have in and around the garden. The barn swallow feeds exclusively on insects: flies, mosquitoes, codling and cutworm moths, weevils, wasps, and bees. They build mud nests and will be attracted to a plank shelf under the eaves of a roof. They will also nest in the rafters of open structures like barns. The tree swallow has a primary diet of insects, though it may also feed on berries. Place a house for them near a marsh or pond and mount it on a pole 3 or 4 feet above the water. A nest box made from a hollowed-out gourd is often a successful attraction. You can grow these fancy gourds in your own garden.

Woodpeckers are great insect hunters, and any of the 17 or more species found in the United States are good to have around the garden. They will feed on ants, aphids, beetles, caterpillars, moths, scales, and snails. If cavities in old trees are not available, they will sometimes use a nest box mounted high in a tree. Do not mount it on your house, or the birds may wake you with their hammering in search of insects!

Wrens are tiny birds that like tiny nest boxes (which they defend aggressively), and they are avid hunters of insects, including ants, beetles, moths, flies, lice, and snails, in the garden.

AMPHIBIANS AND REPTILES

Toads, lizards, salamanders, snakes, and turtles are terrific allies against damaging insects. Many people have a natural aversion to these cold-blooded creatures, but with the exception of a very few venomous snakes, organic gardeners should do everything possible to attract them into the garden. Learn the names of your local species—a natural history society or a field guide will help you—because being able to identify a creature and knowing something about its habits will help you to accept it.

Toads are determined insect eaters. In the cool of night, they will hunt worms, beetles, grubs, and even slugs. You can create a small habitat for them near your garden. They like moist, cool areas (a small water garden is ideal) and will shelter during the day under logs or in piles of old flowerpots. A heavy flowerpot with an entrance cut in one side that is pushed into the ground in a shady spot may persuade them to spend more time in your garden. Some garden catalogs offer toad houses.

Salamanders and **lizards** eat a variety of small insects. If you make a water garden for toads, place some heavy logs and rocks in a damp place nearby; salamanders and lizards might move in. Once you have provided

Salamanders can be differentiated from lizards by their lack of scales and claws.

the right environment for them, you can collect toads and salamanders from the wild to import into your garden. Local natural history buffs and children are usually willing accomplices for such a hunt.

Snakes have a bad reputation that is largely undeserved. Because of this, thousands of harmless and beneficial snakes are brutally slaughtered. Very few are dangerous to man—most notably rattlesnakes, copperheads, water moccasins, and coral snakes—and it's easy to learn to identify any of these that are known in your area. The rest are shy, even timid, and are great hunters of moles, voles, mice, and rats, as well as a variety of insects. The snake most commonly found in gardens is the garter snake. Learn to recognize this one, then work up from there.

Turtles are very beneficial in a garden. Famously slow-moving, they nevertheless manage to catch and eat slugs and a variety of insects. You

BATS IN THE GARDEN

Our human instincts drive us to regard bats as repellent. Vampire myths and scary stories of bat-infested crypts have a lot to do with that. But in the garden and around the yard, it's hard to find a more beneficial creature. Essentially harmless to humans (they can bite if cornered, but who can blame them?), they are voracious consumers of night-flying insects, a category that includes some of the most harmful garden pests as well as mosquitoes. An individual bat can eat 3,000 insects a night. The common brown bat may eat up to half its body weight in insects in one night's feeding.

Contrary to myth, bats are not rodents, don't carry rabies any more than any other species, don't get tangled in people's hair, and are not blind. Before you even consider killing a bat, you should know that of the 43 species of bat found in the United States, 16 are on the endangered species list. If one blunders into your house, please don't panic and scream because that will only confuse the bat more. Open all the windows, turn out or dim the lights, and close the door. If you have to catch a bat, wait until it settles. Wear thick gloves and use a pillowcase or sack to trap it. Carry it outside gently, and release it. This tiny creature is much more frightened of you than you are of it.

Let reason and self-interest overcome any squeamishness you may have, and put up two or three bat houses around your yard. These are available from several mail-order sources, or if you are at all handy you can make your own. Bat Conservation International (Austin, Texas) can provide more information (see page 95).

may catch them to import into your garden, but they are wanderers by nature. Unless you have a large and tightly fenced yard, it's hard to keep them from waddling away, and it's unkind to confine them in too small a space. They may occasionally munch on a vegetable leaf, but such minor damage is nothing compared with their helpful consumption of insects.

MAMMALS

Moles and voles can be a real problem in a garden. Because of this, there seem to be as many "guaranteed" remedies as there are moles and voles. Some people swear by shaving cream squirted in the tunnels, while others use ExLax. Empty plastic bottles buried in the runs, with the necks exposed, are supposed to make a whistling noise that they find abhorrent. And there are any number of electronic noisemakers and vibrators on the market. You can take your pick of these, or resort to common mousetraps set under flowerpots by entrance holes. Be very cautious with poisons, however: pets and harmless wildlife can become the victim if they eat the poison directly or catch and eat the poisoned pest.

RACCOONS AND SQUIRRELS: Anyone who tries to keep a raccoon out of a chicken house or a garbage can soon develops a reluctant respect for their nimble fingers. If you believe that animals cannot reason, watch a raccoon figure out how to open a supposedly raccoon-proof latch. To protect sweet corn, which raccoons love, some beleaguered gardeners leave radios tuned to rock stations blaring all night. Others use motion-sensor floodlights. Once the novelty wears off, however, raccoons will ignore the music and welcome the thoughtfully provided light. If you cannot outwit them, humane trapping in a Havahart trap may be the only answer, followed by a long-distance trip into the woods.

Squirrels can be very cute unless they are monopolizing your bird feeder or chomping on your sweet corn. Determined climbers and incredible leapers, they will also do a bit of digging if a fence gets in the way. A humane trap baited with peanut butter followed by a long trip into the woods is the last resort if you just can't take it anymore. However, please do not trap a squirrel in spring or fall, when it may have dependent babies in its nest.

DEER: Deer have become very destructive garden pests in many areas of the country. Development and hunting have just about extin-

guished their natural predators, but deer have adapted to living in close proximity to humans. Much too close, in the opinion of some gardeners. Deer will walk up steps onto the deck of a house in broad daylight to munch on a tasty potted ornamental. They will jump over moderately high fences to demolish a whole crop of lettuce. And they will denude a perennial border while your friendly dog watches. People have tried lights, noisemakers, and blaring radios, as

Prior to sunrise and just after sunset are when deer normally feed.

well as such exotic deterrents as barbershop hair or coyote urine—even human urine—without long-term success.

What *does* work are special high deer fences, which can be almost (but not quite) invisible, and *serious* electric fences. To reduce the expense of high deer fencing, you can choose to protect only part of your yard; try to design it so that you don't have to open and close gates to drive your car in and out of your property. Electric fencing, properly designed for deer and professionally installed, also works. But don't waste money on the average hardware or farm store electric fencing. Deer sniff at it and walk right through (or under, or over) it. You need the real thing, such as that sold by Premier Fence Systems (Washington, Iowa) to ranchers and livestock breeders (see page 96).

RABBITS: Rabbits are more of a hassle than a pest, because they are relatively easy to keep out of your garden. If they find a way in, however, they can do a lot of damage. If you remember that they can dig holes, you're well on the way to beating them. Install 24-inch or 36-inch small-mesh wire fencing, with the bottom buried 8 to 10 inches in the ground. Best of all, slope the buried part so that it's outside the vertical part of the fence. Rabbits are not bright, so they'll walk up to a fence, sniff it, and start digging right there. If they come up against buried wire mesh, it doesn't occur to them to back off a foot or so and try again. They will give up, and you've won.

Learning to live with wildlife in the garden can be a battle of wits. Be creative, kind, and remember that balance is what it's all about. A healthy ecosystem has room for every sort of creature because Nature intended it to be that way.

SOIL ANALYSIS FOR ORGANIC GROWING

GROWER

SIZE OF GARDEN (ft. by ft.)

SIZE OF FARM (lawn/turf; ft. by ft.)

NO. OF ACRES (landscape; ft. by ft.)

Parts per million (PPM) / 1 PPM = 2 pounds per acre Note: An acre of soil 6-8 inches deep weighs 2,000,000 lbs.

SOIL TEST RESULTS	DESIRED LEVELS
ORGANIC MATTER _____ %	5% Min.
SOIL pH: ▪ acid	
▪ neutral	
▪ alkaline	
MAJOR NUTRIENTS	
Nitrogen/N _____ PPM	250 to 1,500 PPM
N Release/Humus _____ %	5% per year
Phosphorus/P-1 _____ PPM	50 or more PPM
P-Reserve/P-2 _____ PPM	55 or more PPM
Potassium/K _____ PPM	150 to 200 PPM
SECONDARY NUTRIENTS	
Calcium/Ca _____ PPM	750 to 2,000 PPM
Magnesium/Mg _____ PPM	150 to 250 PPM
Sulfur/S _____ PPM	10 to 30 PPM
Sodium/Na _____ PPM	1 to 1,000 PPM
Hydrogen/H _____ MEG	10 MEG/100 grams of soil
MICRONUTRIENTS	
Zinc/Zn _____ PPM	5/8 PPM
Manganese/Mn _____ PPM	25/50 PPM
Iron/Fe _____ PPM	18/50 PPM
Copper/Cu _____ PPM	1.5/2.5 PPM
Boron/B _____ PPM	1.3/2.5 PPM
Molybdenum/Mo _____ PPM	2/7 PPM
Cation Exchange	
Capacity _____ C.E.C.	10/25 (below 10-low; 10-15 ideal above 20-soil problem

C.E.C. = Nutrient Holding Capacity

SOIL TEST RESULTS

PERCENT % BASE SATURATION ACTIVITY

▪ Potassium/K	_____ %	Not Applicable
▪ Magnesium/Mg	_____ %	"
▪ Calcium/Ca	_____ %	"
▪ Sodium/Na	_____ %	"
▪ Hydrogen/H	_____ %	"

DESIRED LEVELS

NUTRIENT RATIOS

N:S Ratio	_____	1:10
P-1:P-2 Ratio	_____	2:1
K:Ca Ratio	_____	10:1
K:Mg Ratio	_____	2:1
Ca:Mg Ratio	_____	Range of 5:1 to 7:1
Mn:Fe Ratio	_____	2:02

MEASURE OF CONDUCTIVITY

Energy Released per gram of soil	_____ ERGS	50-800 ERGS (higher levels are required for top production
Oxygen Reduction Potential	_____ ORP	25 rH (below 25 indicates too much oxygen, resulting in oxidation of organic material and limiting nutrient availability to crops.)

OTHER TESTS

Chlorides	_____ %	**SOIL PARTICLE SIZE:**
Soluble Salts	_____ PPM	▪ Fine
C/N Ratio	_____	▪ Medium
		▪ Large

SOIL TEXTURE

Sand	_____ %	**WATER HOLDING CAPACITY:**
Clay	_____ %	▪ Poor
Loam	_____ %	▪ Fair
		▪ Good

OTHER TESTS

FOLIAR SPRAY PROGRAM
- Every 3 wks.
- Every 5 wks.
- 4 times a season

MICROORGANISMS

Biological Activity:
- Good
- Fair
- Poor
- Bad

Formazan Test for Soil Enzymes:
- Below 100/Poor
- Fair
- Good
- Above 1,000/Excellent

POLLUTANTS TEST

Nitrates/No3	_____ %	Herbicides	_____ %
Fungicides	_____ %	Pesticides	_____ %

HEAVY METALS

Mercury/Hg	_____ PPM	Arsenic/A3	_____ PPM
Cadmium/CD	_____ PPM	Lead/Pb	_____ PPM
Chromium/Cr	_____ PPM	Aluminum/Al	_____ PPM
Nickel/Ni	_____ PPM		

ORGANIC RECOMMENDATIONS AND IMPROVEMENTS

_____
_____
_____
_____
_____
_____
_____
_____
_____
_____

PLANT TISSUE ANALYSIS

GROWER _____

DATE _____

PLANT _____

PLANT TEST RESULTS	DESIRED LEVELS

REFRACTOMETER TEST
(Test for sugar content)   BRIX Reading: Below 6/Poor
Nitrogen/N   _____ %   Above 12/Excellent
Nitrate/No3   _____ %

PLANT PHYTOTOXICITY

Sulfur/S	_____ %	Magnesium/Mg	_____ %
Phosphorus/P	_____ %	Calcium/Ca	_____ %
Potassium/K	_____ %	Sodium/Na	_____ %

CELL INTEGRITY TEST ANALYSIS   CELL INTEGRITY TEST:

Iron/Fe	_____ PPM	▪ Excellent
Manganese/Mn	_____ PPM	▪ Good
Boron/B	_____ PPM	▪ Fair
Copper/Cu	_____ PPM	▪ Poor
Zinc/Zn	_____ PPM	▪ Bad
Aluminum/Al	_____ PPM	
Molybdenum/Mo	_____ PPM	

DEFINITION OF RATINGS

(D) Deficient: Plants should be showing visible symptoms of a nutritional deficiency. Plant growth would definitely be curtailed by an insufficient amount of this element.

(L) Low: Plants may be normal in appearance but probably will be responsive to fertilization with this element.

(S) Sufficient: Plants contain adequate amounts of this element.

(H) High: Optimum yields can be expected.

(E) Excessive: Plants probably show symptoms of a nutritional disorder or stunted growth. Yields may be reduced significantly by an excessive amount of this element.

(N) Nitrogen, (No3) Nitrate, (S) Sulfur, (P) Phosphorus, (K) Potassium, (MG) Magnesium, (Ca) Calcium, (Na) Sodium, (Fe) Iron, (Mn) Manganese, (B) Boron, (Cu) Copper, (Zn) Zinc, (Al) Aluminum, (Mo) Molybdenum

RESOURCES

INFORMATION SOURCES

ATTRA (Appropriate Technology Transfer for Rural Areas)
P.O. Box 3657
Fayetteville, AR 72702
800-346-9140

Bat Conservation International
P.O. Box 162603
Austin, TX 78716-2603
512-327-9721

Bio-Integral Resource Center
Box 7414
Berkeley, CA 94707
510-524-2567

National Pesticide Telecommunications Network Pesticide Hotline
800-858-7378

GARDENING AND PEST CONTROL PRODUCTS

AgriSystems International
125 West 7th Street
Windgap, PA 18091

Arbico
Sustainable Environmental Alternatives for Growers
P.O. Box 4247
Tucson, AZ 85378

D.V. Burrell Seed Growers Co.
P.O. Box 150
Rocky Ford, CO 81067

Charley's Greenhouse Supply
1569 Memorial Highway
Mt. Vernon, WA 98273

Concept, Inc.
213 S.W. Columbia
Bend, OR 97702

Dalen Products
11110 Gilbert Drive
Knoxville, TN 37932

Gardener's Supply Co.
128 Intervale Road
Burlington, VT 05401

Gardens Alive!
5100 Schenley Place
Lawrenceburg, IN 47025

Harmony Farm Supply
P.O. Box 460
Graton, CA 95444

Natural Gardening Company
217 San Anselmo Avenue
San Anselmo, CA 94960

Ohio Earth Food, Inc.
5488 Swamp Street, N.E.
Hartville, OH 44632

Peaceful Valley Farm Supply
P.O. Box 2209
Grass Valley, CA 95945

Premier Fence Systems
Box 89
Washington, IA 52353

Smith & Hawken
25 Corte Madera
Mill Valley, CA 94941

Spalding Laboratories
760 Printz Road
Arroyo Grande, CA 93420

The Urban Farmer Store
2833 Vicente Street
San Francisco, CA 94116

Worm's Way Garden Supply and
   Home Brew Center
3151 South Highway 446
Bloomington, IN 47401

BENEFICIAL INSECTS AND MITES

A-1 Unique Insect Control
5504 Sperry Drive
Citrus Heights, CA 95621

Applied Bionomics Ltd.
11074 West Saanich Road
Sidney, BC V8L 5P5
Canada

Beneficial Insectary
14751 Oak Run Road
Oak Run, CA 96069

Better Yield Insects
RR#3
Site 4, Box 48
Belle River, ON N0R 1A0
Canada

Bio-Control Co.
P.O. Box 337
57A Zink Road
Berry Creek, CA 95916

Biofac
P.O. Box 87
Mathis, TX 78368

BioLogic
P.O. Box 177
Willow Hill, PA 17271

BoBiotrol
54 South Bear Creek Drive
Merced, CA 95340

Bountiful Gardens
18001 Shafer Ranch Road
Willits, CA 95490

Buena Biosystems
P.O. Box 4008
Ventura, CA 93007

W. Atlee Burpee & Co.
300 Park Avenue
Warminster, PA 18974

Foothill Agricultural Research
510½ West Chase Drive
Corona, CA 91720

Fountain Sierra Bug Co.
P.O. Box 114
Rough & Ready, CA 95975

Growing Naturally
P.O. Box 54
Pineville, PA 18946

Hydro-Gardens, Inc.
P.O. Box 9707
Colorado Springs, CO 80932

Nature's Control
P.O. Box 35
Medford, OR 97501

Rincon-Vitova Insectaries, Inc.
P.O. Box 95
Oak View, CA 93022

Stanley Gardens
P.O. Box 913
Belchertown, MA 01007

SOIL TESTING AND TISSUE ANALYSIS

A & L Agricultural Labs
7621 White Pine Road
Richmond, VA 23237

Biosystem Consultants
P.O. Box 43
Lorane, OR 97451

INDEX

Crickets, 81; mole, **58–59,** 71
Crop rotation, 2, **24,** 24–26
Cucumber beetles, 27, 32, *52,* **52–53;**
 control measures for, 69, 73, 74, 76
Cucumber mosaic virus, 52, 53
Cucumbers, 23, 25, 32, 36; companion
 planting with, 27, 28, 29; insects
 harmful to, 27, 32, 52–53, 61, 62, 69,
 73, 74, 76
Cucurbit family, 60, 62. *See also specific
 plants*
Cutworms, 23–24, 30, 39, 53, 53, 84;
 control measures for, 71, 74, 76

D

Daddy longlegs, **47**
Dahlias, 24, 48, 54
Daisies, 41; painted, 24; pyrethrum,
 24, 68
Damsel bugs, **38**
Dandelions, 40
Deer, 79, 80, 88, *88*
Diamondback moths, **53–54,** 71
Diatomaceous earth, 69
Dill, 25, 27, 29, 50; beneficial insects
 attracted to, 37, 40, 43
Disease, 1, 2, 12, 16; biological controls
 and, 71–72; healthy soil as protection
 from, 3–4; spread by insects, 52, 53,
 55, 59
Doodlebugs, 37
Dormant oil, 70, *70*
Double-digging, 12
Dragonflies, **38–39,** 83
Drainage, 7, 9
Drip irrigation, 18, 75
Drought, 17, 18
Dusts. *See* Sprays, dusts, and oils

E

Earthworms, 47
Earwigs, 21, **54,** *54*; control measures
 for, 69, 76
Eelworms, 74
Eggplants, 15, 25, 32, 36, 76; compan-
 ion planting with, 28, 29; insects
 harmful to, 25, 48, 51, 64
Endive, 25
Environmental stress, 17–18
European chafers, 30
European corn borers, 30, **54,** *54*
Evergreens, 49
Evolution, 16, 19
Exoskeletons, 20, 21

F

Fall armyworms, 42, 43, **55,** 71
Fava beans, 39
Feeders, for birds, 81, 87
Fences, 88
Fennel, 27
Fertilizers: organic, 4; synthetic, 4, 16
Feverfew, 24
Figs, 36
Fire ants, 46, **55**
Fireflies, **39**
Fish, 68, 82
Fish extract, *17,* 17–18, *18*
Fish oil spreader-stickers, 72
Flax, 74
Flea beetles, 27, 32, 38, **55,** *55,* 69, 74
Flies, 23, 29, 30, 47; apple maggot, 68,
 77; birds and, 82, 83, 84; blackflies,
 72; blowflies, 36; cabbage-root, 42,
 49–50; carrot rust, 27, 46, **50,** 68, 74;
 cherry fruit, 68; dragonflies, **38–39,**
 83; fireflies, **39;** fruit, 73, 77; green-
 flies, 73; insect adversaries of, 37, 39,
 42; leaf miners, 42, 70; as pollinators,
 35, 36; robber, **42;** sawflies, 30, 83;
 syrphids, **42–43;** tachinid, **43,** *43. See
 also* Whiteflies
Floating row covers, *75,* 75–76
Flower flies, 42–43
Flycatchers, 82
Foliar sprays: for feeding plants, *17,*
 17–18, 18; for insect control, 67–69,
 72–74
Froghoppers (spittle bugs), **62**
Frogs, 41
Frost, 18, 75
Fruit flies, 73, 77
Fruit moths, oriental, 42, **59,** 70, 77
Fruits, 15, 36, 73, 81; companion plant-
 ing with, 24, 27, 28; control measures
 for, 70, 74; insects harmful to, 47,
 59–60, 61, 63. *See also specific fruits*
Fruit tree moths, 74
Fungicides, 4, 16
Funnel-web weavers, **46,** *46*

G

Gardening products, sources for, 90–91
Garden notebooks, 29, 31–32, 66
Garlic, 23, 25, 27, 28, 73, 74
Garter snakes, 86
Genetics, 16–17
Geranium oil, 76
Gnats, 72